THE
MAJEWSKI
CURSE

Dear Lori,
I sincerely hope
you enjoyed the story
my Beautiful friend

Love
Lisa D.
McInnes

LISA DIANNE MCINNES

The Majewski Curse
Copyright © 2021 by Lisa Dianne McInnes

Tellwell Talent
www.tellwell.ca

ISBN
978-0-2288-5988-8 (Hardcover)
978-0-2288-5736-5 (Paperback)
978-0-2288-5735-8 (eBook)

Contents

Prologue

I've wanted to write this story for a long time, but it took years before I could sit down and attempt to write it. However, this story warrants attention, and I'm the only one left to tell it. The awful truth about life is that it is often crueler than fair. It can leave us without choices or a clear path to help handle what gets thrown our way. If these events didn't happen to my own family, I would find them hard to believe. Between the years 2012 and 2017, like a pile of dominos, I watched life take away my loved ones, one by one.

My family's story is one of loss, tragedy, and deception, as well as survival and healing. After enduring severe survivor's guilt, I now have a tremendous appreciation for the fragility of life and recognize the importance of both physical and mental health. Realizing just how vulnerable we all are has helped me understand what being "awakened" truly means. There is no better way to describe how this experience changed me. Though it took a lot of work to get here, I hope my story can help others understand this for themselves.

We are just beginning to understand the connection between the mind and body and the power it wields. I have witnessed, first-hand, how intense stress and toxic emotions can take a toll on both our bodies and minds. My stepson Brandon Majewski's death affected my family in different ways, but I don't doubt that complicated grief and depression played a role in both Devon and Derek Majewski's deaths.

When trauma and unresolved grief disrupt the flow of life, we can lose control of our minds. With every heartbreak, setback, and loss, we seem to sink deeper into the dark water. However, after everything I endured, I knew I had no choice but to choose to heal, with or without my loved ones.

Healing was not straightforward and was much easier said than done. Losing loved ones is one of the most overwhelming experiences of being human—nothing compares to it. Nevertheless, life marches on whether we walk along with it, and whether we choose to die inside or move on is up to us.

Today, small things like sunsets, staring out at the water, and kisses for no reason are the reasons I smile. It is the simple memories that define us and those we hold close to our hearts.

This is the story of the separate yet intertwined tragedies of Brandon, Devon, and Derek Majewski's deaths and the conspiracies that surrounded their family's search for truth.

---◦◦◦〇◦◦◦---

Brandon Majewski's death made headlines when a police officer's wife struck him and his two friends with her vehicle. It was later revealed that the driver, Sharlene Simon, was texting and driving. This issue was compounded by flawed police investigations, which disturbed thousands of those living in Brandon's hometown of Innisfil, Ontario. News of the tragedy spread worldwide after Sharlene decided to sue all three families, eighteen months after the accident. What's more, during the time of Sharlene's lawsuit, we lost our other son, Devon.

I will always wonder what Brandon and Devon would have looked like as grown men and what would have become of their lives. Brandon, who died at seventeen, was 5'9" with an athletic build and had tousled, blonde shoulder-length hair, big blue eyes, and a giant smile. His laugh and voice were loud and boisterous, just like him. He was forever curious, innovative, and loved adventure. There was nothing he set his mind to he didn't achieve.

Devon, the oldest, was twenty-three when he died. He was Brandon's opposite in every way. He was tall and lanky and had short dark-brown hair, deep, soulful brown eyes, and wore thin black glasses. Devon was cautious, conservative, and soft-spoken. He had a great sense of humor and loved to make people laugh.

I will never forget Brandon and Devon and how they impacted my life with their unique and beautiful personalities.

The Accident

October 28th, 2012

You know that feeling you get when you can't make sense of anything, and you feel as though you might be in an episode of *The Twilight Zone*? That's how I felt on October 28th, 2012—the night my life changed forever. It was the beginning of a tsunami of loss that I nor anyone else could ever have predicted.

The chilling cacophony of fists pounding on the door and dogs barking wildly in the middle of the night still haunts me to this day. Not to mention the heart-stopping fear that gripped my heart as my feet hit the floor, and I ran around the house madly, acting solely on instinct, turning on the lights and chasing the horrific sounds, with my mind fleeing nervously from one thought to the next.

When my husband, Derek, and I eventually made it to the main entrance of our home—in what seemed like an eternity amid our disoriented sleep—we realized the hollow pounding was coming from the garage. Evidently, the ringing of the front doorbell had not roused us, so the relentless reverberating sound continued until we finally opened the garage door and were confronted with every parent's worst nightmare.

Red and blue sirens flashed violently before our eyes and blinded us. We stood in shock in front of several police officers as fear took over our bodies.

Nothing could have prepared us for what came next.

"There has been an accident, and we need you to come to the hospital immediately," one of the police officers said. We continued to stand in silence, barely registering his words. "Your son, Brandon, is on life support; you need to hurry." An unforgettable chill ran down my spine.

I immediately raced down the hallway to find clothes, but as I looked back, I could see Derek standing motionless in the hallway. "Hurry up and get dressed!" I yelled like a maniac. However, he didn't budge. I couldn't understand what he was doing, so I screamed once again, "Move, we have to go!"

He then calmly turned toward me, and with tears falling down his face, said, "It doesn't matter, Lisa; he's already dead."

His words infuriated me beyond comprehension, but all I could do was wail, "He is not! Now, hurry up!"

Little did I know that what we would soon discover would forever alter our lives and destroy our family in unimaginable ways.

The drive to the hospital was utter agony. I needed to break the news to Venetta, Brandon's biological mother, as Derek drove, unable to speak. But how could I possibly tell her? Venetta and I have never been close, and as the step-mother, I wasn't sure it was my place. However, I had no other choice, and she needed to know right away.

After three attempts, Venetta finally picked up the phone. I almost felt relieved when she didn't answer on my first two tries. I didn't know how I could tell her without falling apart myself. I was desperately trying to stay calm for Derek.

"Venetta, there has been an accident," I began, then heard her shriek and start to cry on the other end, which immediately sent me into panic mode.

"Please meet us at RVH," I managed to muster. RVH is the Royal Victoria Health Center in Barrie, Ontario, about fifteen minutes from our home in Innisfil. I couldn't bring myself to tell her Brandon was on life support, despite her pleading. I didn't want to be the one to tell her the soul-shattering news. She would discover it soon enough on her own.

After I hung up, I couldn't restrain myself anymore and broke down, realizing what we were about to endure.

I felt numb as we pulled into the parking lot. I don't recall Derek parking the car but would come to realize later that we had absentmindedly parked in the middle of the emergency lot.

We ran into the hospital, taken over by the rush of adrenaline, and frantically searched the waiting room. The woman behind the desk stood up, so I went over to her and explained what had happened.

She immediately asked for a name. "Brandon Majewski," I said in a panic. Her eyes grew wider, and I instantly perceived a hint of sadness in them.

At that moment, Venetta ran through the sliding doors, sobbing and visibly shaken. "Where is he?" she exclaimed.

The nurse came forward, and we followed her down the corridor in a blind trance, desperately trying to process what had happened. When we reached the end of the hall, she ushered us into a small white room and told us she would take us to see Brandon shortly.

I looked over at Derek and noticed he had begun to cry uncontrollably. "I've been in one of these rooms before," he finally said through sobs. "This is where they take you when someone has died."

Just then, the nurse opened the door, and with a look of deep concern on her face, said, "I'm sorry," then paused for a moment and continued, "whoever informed you that your son was on life support was mistaken. I don't know how to say this, but the truth is, he broke his neck and didn't make it to the hospital alive. I'm so sorry. He's gone."

Numbness spread over me, and I couldn't process what was happening. My seventeen-year-old step-son was gone, and my husband and his ex-wife were in hysterics. Our collective sobs reverberated throughout the room as we unanimously groped for air. No words could express the sheer sadness we all felt at that moment.

Once we caught our breath, the nurse asked if we wanted to see Brandon but recommended against doing so. "He's covered in bruises, and you will find him virtually unrecognizable," she said, then explained it would be better to remember him as he was, and we all agreed.

After an indefinite amount of time, a police officer knocked on the door and came into the room. He introduced himself, then said, "I want to start by saying how very sorry I am for your loss." He stood in silence for a moment. We thanked him for his condolences, then waited for him to proceed. He cleared his throat and began, "The woman who killed your son feels terrible about it." We looked at him in shock. "She is beside herself and is practically inconsolable," he added.

The room became deathly quiet. We could not believe what we were hearing. Had we misheard him? We looked around at each other, perplexed. Was he trying to elicit sympathy for our son's killer? Wait, What?

It was one of those moments one can't forget, a significant point that cannot be erased. Something didn't feel right, and even though I didn't understand it at the time, we later learned what the officer meant.

The Beginning

I met Brandon and Devon Majewski's father, Derek Majewski, at a Halloween party in September 2003, one year after I had separated from my children's father.

My first thought when I first saw Derek was that he looked intelligent and scholarly. He also had a great smile and made me feel at ease from the get-go.

Derek was 43 years old, 5'11", with short medium-length brown hair, and big brown eyes. He wore round glasses, a suit and tie, and had a wicked sense of humor, which was a prerequisite for me. Derek had a background in chemical engineering and had been working at a company called General Filtration in Vaughan, Ontario, for about ten years. He loved his job and colleagues. They were a tight-knit group, and he considered them family. He was hard-working, responsible, and a family man who genuinely cared for the people close to him. I was instantly attracted to how open and honest he was about everything in his life, including his struggles.

Derek had lost both his parents for entirely different reasons and at separate times. He told me he had lost his father to lung cancer, which, as painful as it was, didn't come as a surprise since his father was a long-time smoker. However, what happened to his mother was a different story. The year before we met, Derek's mother, Heidi, was set to move in with him to help care for his sons, Devon and Brandon. She had just lost her husband of 45 years and was alone in the world.

When Derek told me the story of his mother's death, I was horrified. It's one of those stories of misfortune you'd never think could happen to you or someone you know. It was heartbreaking to listen to him relate what happened. The shadow of pain across his face was evident.

In the summer of 2001, Heidi Majewski went in for routine gallbladder surgery, and although she returned to Derek's home post-op, she never woke up the following day. The operating surgeon accidentally nicked her intestine, and she died in her sleep of sepsis. While the mortality rate of routine operations is low, and a surgeon may successfully perform the surgery thousands of times, each patient is different. What happened to Heidi was exceptionally unusual and rare, and unfortunately, she was one of the few unlucky ones. Derek said his mother pulled an "unlucky lottery ticket." I later learned that bitter sarcasm was a big part of Derek's personality; it was his way of coping with situations that caused him pain or distress.

I didn't realize at the time that what happened to Derek's mother, his children, and later, what happened to him, would haunt me in nightmares, causing me to suffer from severe insomnia. Years later, I would lay awake in the middle of the night, wondering whether any of us had control over our lives or if our lives were predetermined. Most importantly, I'd question whether there was such a thing as a family curse.

Before meeting me, Derek married his high school sweetheart, Venetta, a former college instructor in Mississauga, Ontario. They were together for twenty years and had Devon and Brandon. Derek mentioned their marriage should have ended sooner as they had several marital problems they could not reconcile.

Despite having various issues. He also added that he felt pressure from his parents, who told him that "family was everything" and divorce should not be an option when there are children involved, very old-school European values.

However, years after Brandon was born, Derek told me that Venetta no longer wanted to stay in the marriage and it ended abruptly.

Derek had deeply-rooted trust issues, that seemed to revolve around deception when I met him, and they were apparent right away. His marriage had left scars and he explained how their problems had caused a strain not only between them but their entire family as the kids—mainly Devon—watched the family fall apart.

Devon, who was twelve years old at the time, was mature enough to understand the issues his parents were having, and it deeply affected him. He was a highly sensitive boy with a noticeable dark side, which I picked up on right away. I presumed it was a consequence of having to process too much too soon. However, as we got closer, I became somewhat of a therapist and older sister figure to him, someone he could trust and feel safe to confide in his deepest fears and secrets. As an adolescent, I had a strained relationship with my mother, so I understood the pain he felt and what it meant to pretend everything was okay and feel torn inside.

On the other hand, Brandon was only six years old when his parents separated, it would always appear that Brandon remained closer to his mother, and Devon closer to his dad.

Derek would often say that everything happens for a reason and always said that had his marriage ended earlier, Brandon would never have been born, had that been the case, I would not be telling this story right now . . .

After the divorce, Venetta moved to Brampton, and this is when Brandon and Devon were separated from each other. Devon fought to stay with his dad. He went before a judge, and Derek obtained full-time custody. Brandon stayed with his mom, but Derek was given 50/50 custody, seeing him one week on and one week off. Devon's relationship with his step-father George was tense, and his visits to his mother's house were rare because of it.

When we first met, Derek was living in Mississauga, about half an hour away from Brampton, with fourteen-year-old Devon and eight-year-old Brandon in the house he and his father had built from the ground up many years before. He had a nanny/ house-keeper to help with the chores, as well as Brandon. Derek realized he had bitten off more than he could chew with having Brandon one week on and one week off and was finding it stressful. However, he didn't want to give up seeing him, so he struggled along, as his children meant the world to him, a quality that I admired greatly.

The boys grew up in Mississauga and Devon's childhood best friend, Darren, lived next door. Darren would later play a notably tragic part in Devon's death.

I lived in Brantford, Ontario—about an hour from Mississauga—when I met Derek. I lived in a house on a quiet street with my two very young children, Christopher and Angelina. My oldest, Christopher, was three years old, with dark brown hair, laughing brown eyes, and endless energy. Everyone always used to say he looked like a little "Harry Potter" since he wore round glasses. My youngest, Angelina, was one and a half years old, with light brown hair, gorgeous brown eyes, a round face, and a sweet disposition. She was a happy little girl who stole everyone's heart with her charming smile.

I was twenty-nine years old and energetic. I was working two jobs to pay my mortgage and bills, which did not leave me with enough time for a personal life.

However, I had a fulfilling life and wondered whether I was interested in bringing anyone into my children's lives at all. Dating is different when there are young children involved, and the idea certainly made me nervous. I was determined never to get divorced again, so whoever I got involved with needed to be a family man since that was the bone of contention with my previous husband. My children rarely saw their father after the divorce, so I decided that if anyone new was to ever come into our lives, it would be imperative he accepts my children as his own.

I worked in an office in the accounting department at a large company during the day and bartended at a nightclub in Burlington called Splash on the weekends for extra money and a little socializing. For me, it was a win-win; I had the perks of a social life while getting paid.

After my divorce, my aunt moved in with me. She had been living alone for quite some time and was grateful for the companionship she received from the children and me. She had worked as a nanny in her younger years, so I knew my children were in good hands. I was so appreciative to have her around; I could earn a living with peace of mind, knowing my kids were safe and sound.

Six months after we met, Derek and I decided the distance between us was becoming a strain, and since we wanted to make our relationship work and loved spending time together, we decided to put both our houses up for sale and move in together.

Derek's house sold quickly, and he swiftly found us a three-bedroom condo in Mississauga large enough for all of us to temporarily move into after my home in Brantford sold. Christopher, Angelina, and I moved in with Derek and Devon and began to look for a place to live that would work for everyone. As beautiful as the condo was, we all needed more space to roam.

Hamilton, 2005

After selling the condo, we moved into a beautiful five-bedroom home in a quiet cul-de-sac that backed onto a large park in Hamilton. Logistically, it was the perfect choice for us. Derek had a decent commute to Mississauga, and I was close to my family in Cambridge. The area was about ten-minutes from Ancaster, a former municipality in Hamilton located on the Niagara Escarpment. It was secluded yet close to everything, and it was a five-minute walk to the local high and elementary schools. Hamilton was also central to Brandon, who continued to live with Venetta in Brampton, so his visits remained the same, and he stayed with us every weekend.

At this time, Devon was sixteen, Brandon was ten, Christopher was six, and Angelina was three. It was a glorious time in all their lives, and it made my heart infinitely happy to see that everyone got along so well. It was as though they had been siblings all along. Devon and Brandon always looked out for young Christopher and Angelina.

Moving was the hardest on Devon. As a sixteen-year-old high school student, changing schools and making friends was not an easy task. He had lived in Mississauga his whole life, so Hamilton proved to be somewhat of a culture shock for him.

In the end, Devon did a phenomenal job of making new friends and blending in. It wasn't in his nature to make friends with everyone, but he was lucky enough to make a few lasting friendships and even managed to get a part-time job at a local drug store.

Christopher made fast friends with Ryan, the boy who lived two doors down, and they remain friends to this day. His parents, Christine and Steven, would come to be great friends of mine. They were two of the kindest people I have ever met, and later in life, when I would need someone to depend on, they would be there for me.

Angelina was still very young and was not in school. She befriended a little girl who lived across the street named Cassandra, and they rode their bikes around our cul-de-sac all day long, going back and forth between our house and hers for popsicles and playtime.

Derek continued to work for General Filtration but had been entertaining an offer to work for his friend Lou at Fil-trek, a company within the same field of business in Cambridge, Ontario—a mere forty-minute drive from Hamilton. He made Derek an offer he couldn't refuse, which included a new Mercedes and a very substantial pay raise. However, the job required Derek to travel across Canada and the United States two to three weeks out of the month. After much deliberation, Derek decided it was time for a change and took the job. In the meantime, I took care of the house and our four kids and ran a small daycare business out of our home.

Hamilton, 2007

Two years after we moved to Hamilton, Brandon, who was twelve at the time, came to live with us full-time. He missed Devon and loved being a big brother to Christopher and Angelina. He enjoyed the camaraderie of a large family unit and living with Venetta and George provided a different dynamic.

Therefore, it came as no surprise when Brandon called in the middle of the night to have Derek pick him up, stating he wanted to come and live with us.

When Brandon came to live with us, we quickly realized how different he was from the other children. He lacked the ability to understand language and writing but had an astute capacity for reasoning and analysis. Brandon understood complicated puzzles and could take the toaster apart and put it back together. He had a unique way of looking at the world and could hyper-focus on the things that interested him. His friends loved being around him. His gregarious, excited demeanor and endless curiosity were contagious, just like the smile he always had on his face.

At school, his teachers took notice. Although he wasn't book smart, they told us that he had an extraordinary mind and could think outside the box, unlike the other students. His science teacher believed Brandon's inclination for the unconventional would serve him in the future, and he'd invent something useful.

When Brandon was in the third grade, he was diagnosed with attention deficit hyperactivity disorder (ADHD). However, it was later determined—during his teens—that he also had high-functioning autism or Asperger's syndrome, as well as obsessive-compulsive disorder (OCD). Nevertheless, these disorders did not hinder him in any way. Instead, they complemented his ADHD and kept him focused on his interests. No matter what he set his mind to, he would obsess over it until he was satisfied with the result.

Brandon was never interested in playing with toys; instead, he was much more interested in learning how things worked and what made them work. He'd watch the *Discovery Channel* and David Suzuki's *The Nature of Things*, then recreate what he'd seen. Brandon would find and collect stuff others didn't want—garbage he could salvage—and use the parts to create something new. He never understood why people threw perfectly useful things away. For his birthday and Christmas, Brandon always asked for money. At first, I found it strange but later realized he was forward-thinking enough to save his money to fund whatever project he had in the works. When he was ten years old, Brandon created a YouTube webpage called *High Voltage Science,* where he'd post some of his beginner experiments. Later, his experiments evolved, and I began to realize he was bound for great things.

Brandon built his first major project when he was twelve years old and had just moved in with us. I watched as he tacked his engineered drawings to the wall and accumulated used parts, epoxy, wood, and tools in our garage.

We didn't know what he was working on, and he told us it was a secret, but a few weeks later, once the project started taking shape, we realized he was building a boat. "It's going to be a sea flea," he told me. I had never heard of a sea flea boat before but learned it was a small motorized boat made of plywood. Brandon worked on the boat day and night until it was completed and he was ready to test its seaworthiness.

We spent many summers at Lovesick Lake, a beautiful lake about two and a half hours away from Hamilton, nestled in the north of Ontario. Our place was right across the water, and I would spend my days watching the kids play and fish on the dock that stretched over the rippling waves.

The day came for the launch of Brandon's sea flea boat. The kids gathered around the dock, anxious to see whether Brandon's creation would float. We watched in amazement as the kids gave the boat a final push and it slid into the water with Brandon at the helm. He cranked the motor rigorously, then off he went, instantly speeding across the water with his blonde hair blowing back in the wind and a proud smile across his face. I couldn't help but smile as a sense of pride filled me. Here was a twelve-year-old kid who built his own boat with his own hands. This would be the beginning of many projects to come.

In 2011, six years after we moved to Hamilton, the city's crime rate increased and became prevalent, causing the communities to act. One of the mothers at Brandon's school told me that her teenage son was jumped and beaten by two boys while walking home through a park not far from home and not far from where we lived. Other stories like this one came out and sent Derek into a panic. Brandon was sixteen years old now and an accomplished rider of just about anything, especially his unicycle. Since Brandon was now old enough to wander around town on his own, Derek was worried something might happen to him as Brandon was a trusting and friendly kid. It wasn't uncommon for Brandon to wind up in a neighbor's living room without telling anyone. More than once, we thought he'd gone missing only to find him talking about his latest project with a relative stranger.

Derek decided it was time to move to a smaller town for the kids' sake. We started our search almost immediately and discovered a little town located on the western shore of Lake Simcoe in Simcoe County, Ontario, called Innisfil, with a population of 36,000. Innisfil was hours away from everyone we knew, and although I was apprehensive about moving there at first, it was precisely what we were looking for—a quaint area with a small-town feel. Brandon was over the moon at the idea of snowmobiling, seadooing, and having a beach in the backyard. We wasted no time in putting the house in Hamilton up for sale, and it sold within six days of being on the market. Now, it was time to find a home in Simcoe County. Innisfil didn't have a variety of houses to choose from as residential development was only beginning to expand. We saw numerous houses in the middle of town, but we wanted to be within walking distance of the beach. One day, while driving around in the rain, we found a beautiful home, complete with a lush backyard, an immense vegetable garden, and only steps away from the lake and beach. The house was not as impressive as the others we had looked at, but it felt like home.

Innisfil, 2011

We moved into our new home in Innisfil on December 15th, 2011. It was the dead of winter, but thankfully, the typical eight-inch-plus snowfall had not yet arrived, so the movers managed to get the job done with minor issues.

Innisfil was a picturesque community, with quiet streets, no highways or road noise, and the lake five houses down at the end of our street. The city itself was a little far from any major shopping centers and conveniences, but that could be a good thing sometimes.

I had often heard stories about how people in small towns were uniquely friendly, but nothing could prepare us for the warm welcome we received.

When we pulled into the driveway on Taylorwoods Boulevard and got the kids out of the car, our next-door neighbors on the left came over and introduced themselves. They were a young couple in their forties, with two children. The husband was a Brampton district police officer, and his wife was a nurse. I specifically remember thinking they were the perfect neighbors to have in an emergency. Little did I know I would later seek their aid. After extending their welcome, they offered to help us unpack and feed us after a long day.

More neighbors came by throughout the day with balloons, cookies, and fruit baskets. Our neighbors to our house's right were a local elementary school teacher and an engineer with teenage children. We later learned they hosted an annual Easter egg hunt in their enormous backyard for all the kids on the street. I remember thinking how quaint everything seemed. The fascinating part was that the entire street amounted to people from various parts of the Greater Toronto Area, the most populous metropolitan area in Canada, who wanted to get away from city life and create a simpler environment for themselves and their families.

The hospitality was overwhelming, to say the least, and we felt at home right away. Any doubt I might have had initially about moving to Innisfil began to melt away.

Everyone was happy except Devon, who was now twenty-two years old and had left behind his new friends from Hamilton. Luckily, they all drove and would come to visit him on the weekends.

Brandon, who was now sixteen, was in his glory. He promptly made plans for beach-side activities and immediately turned our new garage into a construction zone for his latest projects.

Brandon soon made a name for himself in the neighborhood with his latest invention. He took a weed whacker motor, attached it to the back of his bicycle, and turned his ordinary bike into a motorized one. It wasn't long before a steady lineup of kids stood in front of our garage, eagerly waiting for Brandon to show them how they could do the same. Brandon was ecstatic. He loved to show others his new projects and teach them how to re-create his inventions. As news got around, Brandon met Randy, a fifteen-year-old boy who lived around the corner. He had feathered brown hair and big, honest blue eyes, just like Brandon. The two clicked immediately, mainly due to their mutual interest in creating experiments, blowing stuff up, and anything with a loud motor. Later, Brandon made friends with Richard, an adventurous boy from school. The two would go on various adventures around the neighborhood and try new things.

In the short time we had lived in Innisfil, Brandon accumulated two snowmobiles and a Sea-Doo from Kijiji—an online platform that allows people to exchange goods and services. Brandon slowly took over the garage once again, and it now consisted of cars, bikes, a unicycle, a SeaDoo, two snowmobiles, and a Tesla coil—an electric resonant transformer circuit. Brandon had been researching Nikola Tesla for a while, and his most recent invention was going to be to build a Tesla coil in time for Halloween.

Before long, I learned that Brandon would do most things only to see if he could. He never started a project without finishing it. Angelina loved to watch as he worked on his creations in the garage and would sometimes take on the role of his assistant.

Christopher, who was now twelve, and Angelina, who was now nine, were equally excited about their new start. They frantically ran all over the house, arguing about who would get the bigger bedroom, as kids always do.

When Halloween finally arrived, Brandon's Tesla coil was ready. He called us to the garage and could barely contain his excitement. The Tesla coil was a huge success, and bolts of lightning shot across our driveway. Brandon's Halloween surprise included a life-size Jack the Ripper statue that lit up with flashes of electricity as trick-or-treaters came by the house. It terrified the children, but Brandon was on cloud nine, and all of us were in awe of his latest innovation.

Settling into Innisfil

The first order of business was to decide which schools the children would attend. Both Derek and I came from Catholic upbringings due to our European backgrounds—I am half-Scottish/half-Polish and Derek Polish—but neither of us practiced. The kids had attended Catholic schools in Hamilton, but we let them chose the schools this time since our neighbors' opinions and advice varied greatly.

Brandon chose Nantyr Shores, the local public high school in Innisfil, which was less than a mile away from home, while Christopher and Angelina chose Goodfellow Public School. Their principal gave us a tour and told us a little about the school's history. It was older, but it had been renovated, with a big gymnasium, protected green space, and was two blocks away from home.

Angelina, the social butterfly, fit in right away. On the other hand, being shy and more introverted, Christopher took his time choosing and making new friends. He kept in touch with Ryan, his best friend from Hamilton, and the two would play Xbox Live after school together. I would hear Ryan's voice echo from the system in Christopher's bedroom when he would get home from school, and it put a smile on my face.

Derek continued to commute to his job at Fil-trek. Fortunately, because his work required a lot of travel, he could set his hours within reason. As for me, I started up my daycare service once again and received plenty of responses. In the end, I settled on looking after three children, which was more than enough for me. I was excited about my new start, as was Angelina, who earned some pocket money by helping me before and after school. She loved playing with the toddlers and learned some responsibility along the way. I developed a lesson plan, put insurance in place, and set up a nanny cam so that parents could check in remotely. Our location was stellar, and I would take the kids on daily walks in a triple stroller to the beach and playground, where we would feed the geese.

I was relieved at how quickly the family adapted to our new surroundings and was especially surprised at how well I acclimatized. I had always enjoyed the level of anonymity one maintains in a big city, but the more we settled into our new home, the more I grew to appreciate the informality of small-town living. This was our third move, and I hoped it would be our last. However, although my initial doubts and apprehension about moving had waned, a subtle gut feeling nagged me, which I chalked up to anxiety but would later reconsider.

We settled in quite nicely by Christmastime and had a wonderful first Christmas in our new home. Derek's only sister moved to Costa Rica when her two sons were teenagers, so we always had Derek's nephews over for the holidays. Devon and Brandon loved seeing their cousins, and I had come from a small family, so I enjoyed the camaraderie. Christmases were fun-filled, loud, and boisterous, with a lot of food, presents, and alcohol—mostly vodka for the Polish men in the family. It felt like we were a modern-day "Brady Bunch.", two were his and two were mine.

After Christmas, Devon was set to relocate to Toronto for school to eventually become a paralegal. He would move in with his eccentric eighty-five-year-old great-aunt on Derek's side, who lived alone in a big house downtown. Toronto is about an hour away from Innisfil, so Devon made plans to commute home every weekend by train. Devon was somewhat of a finicky character. I always believed he had a mild case of dystychiphobia—an excessive fear of accidents—and would be overly cautious about everything, especially driving. He was terrified of getting into a car accident and never got his license. When he had turned sixteen, Derek wanted to buy him a car, but Devon refused. Therefore, the idea of living in Toronto and getting around on public transportation suited him.

We were excited for Devon to start this new chapter in his life, and working as a paralegal seemed like a great career choice.

The Curse

T he weekend before he left for Toronto, Devon and I sat in the garage like we had done so many times before while he smoked a cigarette. Devon was in an unusual mood, and although he had somewhat of a paranoid and mysterious personality, today, something was different. "What's wrong?" I asked him. He stared at me for a minute, then said something I wasn't expecting.

"Our family is cursed, you know?" he began. I had become used to Devon's frequent morose moods and therefore assumed he was reacting negatively to leaving home for the first time. "Lisa, it's true. The way my grandmother and uncle from Poland died is not normal." Devon's grandmother died from complications after a routine gall bladder surgery, and his uncle had suffered an unlikely heart attack after his roommates withheld his heart medication from him, a murder of sorts it appeared. It was later supposed that they had done so in the hopes of taking over his property and doctoring the will and documents, something much easier done in Poland. It was a tragic loss indeed and one that was shrouded in mystery.

I sat silently for a minute, feeling uneasy. "Devon," I finally said slowly, "curses don't exist, and even if they did, they would only have power if you believed in them, which I don't, and neither should you." He looked down and didn't respond. I looked at him reassuringly, but he just hung his head lower and gave me a slight nod. I wasn't convinced he believed me, but we never spoke of it again. However, it wouldn't be until much later that Devon's words would come back to haunt me.

Summer in Innisfil was a lot of fun, and we always found something to do with the kids and dogs. We had sold our place on Lovesick Lake when we moved to Innisfil since Lake Simcoe and Innisfil Beach were just minutes away from our new house. Innisfil Beach was breathtaking, and so peaceful, that often, it felt as though we were the only ones there.

Rufus, our miniature collie, loved to play fetch and would run in and out of Lake Simcoe's blue water with a stick for hours. Since the water near the beach was so shallow and felt like bath water, we'd take our shoes off and wade in it and enjoy the view. The kids' favorite part of the summer was buying ice cream from the old-fashioned ice cream truck that made its rounds around our neighborhood and the beach multiple time s a day. Its circus-like melody could be heard from at least a block away, so the kids always had time to look for change before it came around the corner.

The summer marched on, and we all enjoyed having fun in our new country home, and everything Innisfil had to offer. Devon would come home from Toronto on the weekends and tell us stories about life in the big city. Housing and rent were expensive in Toronto, so it made sense that Devon lived with his eighty-five-year-old great-aunt for the two years until he graduated. However, I started to doubt whether he would last to graduation, given his complaints about her constant rants and putdowns. He would say that she had a very negative disposition and would take her moods out on whoever happened to be around, and unfortunately, since he was living with her presently, it was quite often him. She had been married multiple times before, but she had been on her own for quite some time now.

Although he took her tirades in stride, they didn't end with him, he would speak of countless issues she had with her neighbors on both sides, and Devon would find himself watching her domestic battles, often finding them entertaining it seemed, coming home and laughing with Brandon. On one such occasion, to get back at one of her neighbors, she urinated into a bucket and used a Super Soaker to spray her urine through an open window upstairs onto the neighbor's clean laundry hanging to dry on the line outside. If this were anyone else, I would have never believed the story, but since I had the misfortune of meeting her on several occasions and always had the distinct impression something was not right with her, it was easy to believe.

Derek and I would go into the city with Brandon, Christopher, and Angelina to visit Devon and take his great-aunt for dinner. She was not an easy person to be around, and her strict demands left us on pins and needles whenever we were in her presence.

She never had children of her own, so when Derek was young, they shared a close connection. However, several years before Derek and I met, he had a falling out with her, and they were not on speaking terms when we got together. Derek's uncle had died in Poland and had left him some money in his will. However, she had a hard time collecting the money and even misplaced the will at one point. She had accused Derek of breaking into her home and stealing the will until she "found" it again. Eventually, they resumed contact, and despite a lack of apology on her part, Derek kept the family ties alive for Devon and Brandon's sake.

I never understood why she was the way she was. Her sense of entitlement was very confusing, and I often wondered whether she had ever known happiness. Regardless, I understood why Devon was starting to feel miserable living there, there are some people that just suck the life out of the room when you meet them, she was one of them.

The summer was almost over, and the trees began to change color. Soon, it would be time to get the kids ready for back to school. Brandon was going into his last year of high school, Christopher into his first, and Angelina would be going into the sixth grade.

Brandon was now in the beginning stages of yet another invention—a street-legal dirt bike hybrid. He painstakingly ordered the parts one by one and polished the chrome pieces until they shone like mirrors. It was always exciting to watch Brandon start a project and work so methodically until completion. Scott, one of our neighbors who lived by the beach a few houses down, ran a business from home, building custom motorcycles. Brandon would watch him as he worked, and later, Scott helped him put the bike and motor together for his hybrid creation.

I still remember Scott saying, "I hope he doesn't kill himself with this thing." I would laugh as none of us were ever worried about Brandon having trouble riding anything. He could ride a unicycle backward with a friend on his shoulders. Killing himself on anything with two wheels wasn't something that concerned us at all.

Derek continued working from Monday to Thursday and would take long weekends to go fishing with Brandon and Christopher. When Devon was not with us, I would go along with them. Otherwise, Devon and I would spend quality time together since he wasn't too keen on fishing, nor was he the outdoorsy type.

Derek had always been an avid watch collector and had an extensive collection of designer and vintage watches. He knew everything there was to know about them and took pride in his hobby. One weekend, he decided to start a weekend side business selling his watches at the local flea market during the winter months. His best friend, Mark, had made a name for himself at the Mississauga flea market selling jewelry and had been quite successful. I encouraged Derek to set up shop and thought it'd be a great way to earn some extra cash while having some fun.

Brandon had become quite popular around the neighborhood and continued to enjoy a steady stream of local teenagers and children coming to the house, asking to have their bicycles tricked out. He always had parts lying around and was too good-hearted to say no. Eventually, he had converted most of the local kids' bikes, and before long, our community had become a race track. I'd often hear the roaring sound of motorized bikes whizzing by as the kids raced up and down the streets, with Brandon as their leader. He was proud of the legacy he had started, and his sense of accomplishment was evident by the beaming smile across his face.

One day, Brandon received a call from Duffield Sports, a local motorcycle shop, offering him a part-time job to help in the shop. Brandon was ecstatic. His dream was to own a bicycle or motorcycle shop someday, and this proved to be his first step in that direction. He always knew he wanted to be an entrepreneur and believed there was nothing better than getting paid to do something you love.

I related to his aspirations. I came from a family of entrepreneurs, so I encouraged him to pursue his dream of starting his own business. I told him the first step was to choose something he loved and make sure he had the right skills and product people needed.

Brandon was somewhat of an entrepreneur right from the time he was little. He always had his eye on the things others didn't see, and he loved to make money. One night, a neighbor who lived a couple of doors down had thrown out some large items, and Brandon wanted to collect them. I didn't feel good about it. The trash had belonged to the local head of the Parent-Teacher Association, and I didn't want Brandon getting caught lurking through it. I told him he would have to wait until it got late enough so that no one would notice. I had to laugh when it turned out that both items worked fine, and Brandon sold them online for $150. It was moments like these that proved I would never have to worry about Brandon. He was money-savvy and would always find his way in the world. I felt reassured he had a promising life and career ahead of him.

My daycare business was doing well, and I had transformed my basement into a romper room. I was happy to spend my days in shorts and T-shirts, and I would occasionally put on a clown face or costume to entertain the kids. I had added a couple more part-time children before and after school, and Angelina continued to be a great help and support.

The first week after school started, Christopher and Angelina came home with consent forms for trips to Snow Valley Ski Resort. The school had arranged skiing, tubing, and snowboarding outings for the students to attend throughout the winter months. Snow Valley Ski Resort was in Minesing, Ontario, which was about half an hour from Innisfil. Living near the mountains had its perks, and the kids couldn't wait to learn how to ski and snowboard.

Brandon had also become consumed with getting his new snowmobile ready for the winter once he discovered all the local students rode them to school. He couldn't wait to fly through the snow on his way to class.

Derek's booth at the local flea market was doing well, and he had amassed quite a following of loyal customers. People would regularly bring in jewelry they wanted to sell, and he was making a considerable profit, given the relatively small market. He enjoyed his small business a lot more than he thought he would.

Life seemed to be going smoothly for everyone, and I started to think that maybe my initial hesitation about moving had been close-minded. However, the more time we spent in Innisfil, the more I couldn't understand why I was having trouble feeling "at home." We lived in a beautiful neighborhood with great neighbors and community, yet I felt restless and uneasy. Was it just me? Or was there more to it than just missing my friends back home in Hamilton?

It was now almost Halloween once again, and we had begun to deck the house with Halloween decorations. Every year, we would add at least one new item to our collection. This year, Christopher picked out a giant inflatable cat that would sit in the middle of the front lawn. I was never a fan of the inflatable decorations, but the kids loved them.

Brandon set up Jack the Ripper next to Frankenstein on the front porch and, on Halloween night, intended to set up his Tesla coil to scare the trick-or-treaters once again.

The weekend before Halloween, Innisfil held its monthly tween dance at the local elementary school. A local Innisfil resident had started the dances years before when his children were young. He realized there wasn't a lot for the kids to do in town, so he put together a committee that would hold a monthly dance. A $10 admission included four hours of dancing, fun, and friends, as well as a bag of chips and a pop.

This weekend's dance was special because it was Halloween-themed. The excitement level at our house was through the roof as Angelina and Christopher got ready. I was thrilled to help them with their costumes and enjoyed every second of it. I felt like a kid all over again.

This year, Angelina made her costume. She went as Minnie Mouse and looked adorable with her dark hair, long lashes, black nose, and ears. Christopher went as a skeleton. He donned a full-body costume, complete with a hood. The bones lit up and glowed a brilliant green, while the eyes under the hood glowed red.

Derek was coming home from a business trip later that night, so Brandon waited for him to get back before heading to Randy's house to hang out with him. The two were going to put the finishing touches on Randy's new motorbike. I never gave a second thought to Brandon spending time with Randy. His family was amazing, and I loved his parents and sister. They were one of the nicest families I have ever known.

I wasn't home when Derek returned. I had gone to pick up the kids from the Halloween dance, and as usual, it took them some time to find their way to the car, so I went inside and searched for them in the gymnasium. I made my way through the sea of young faces until I found them, and a few minutes later, Christopher, Angelina, and two of their friends piled into our SUV. Their friends were spending the night at our house, so the excitement from the dance and sugar they consumed continued in the car as we drove.

By the time we arrived, Derek was home and relaxing on the couch, with his bags still in the hallway. When the kids walked through the door, he got up, hugged them, and told them how great their costumes looked. They hugged him back and bounced away with their friends to get changed and ready for bed. I told them they could watch a Halloween movie downstairs with some popcorn—but no more sugar.

I asked Derek where Brandon was, and he told me he had left for Randy's place a short while after he got home. He and Brandon had spent some time together watching TV before sending Brandon off with some money for a bite to eat with friends.

Derek was tired, so I helped him unpack his things, and he headed to bed as he had to be up early for the flea market. Even though I sometimes joined him at his booth in the early morning on the weekends, I would always stay up until all the kids were home and in bed. I couldn't sleep properly if any of them were out.

Christopher and Angelina had their sleepover, so they were busy watching the movie downstairs as I sat alone in the living room, reading a book on my iPad.

An hour went by, and Angelina came upstairs to get a drink, and in that instance, the phone rang. We had one of those wall-mounted phones with call display, and when I got up and saw that Brandon's friend, Richard, was calling, I immediately told Angelina not to answer it. Richard was one of Brandon's best friends, but together, they made me nervous for reasons I couldn't explain. There was no reason for me to feel this way; it was just a gut feeling. However, Brandon seemed to enjoy his time with Richard, so it seemed there was no reason to worry.

The phone continued to ring until the answering machine picked it up. Angelina looked at me with confusion, but I couldn't explain why I was averse to answering Richard's call. He was most likely calling to see if Brandon was home, but seeing Richard's name on the call display left me feeling sick and disturbed. I immediately called Brandon's cell phone, but he didn't answer. Brandon didn't like using his cell phone and very rarely answered it. It usually sat buried in his pocket or was uncharged. It drove me crazy; however, he was always good at coming home and checking in.

Richard did not stop at one phone call. He called four more times, and each time, I let it go to voicemail. I felt nauseous and couldn't understand why, but I felt assured in knowing that if I could not get a hold of Brandon, neither could anyone else.

It was getting late, and I was having a hard time getting Christopher, Angelina, and their friends to settle down. I should've known that allowing them both to have a sleepover on the same night was a mistake, but it was Halloween weekend, so I made an exception. It was midnight by the time I managed to get them into bed. By 1 a.m., the house was finally quiet, and I was ready to go to sleep myself.

I'm not altogether sure what happened next as it seemed as though I had just closed my eyes before I was woken up most abruptly and unexpectedly.

I heard fists pounding on the garage door coupled with the ferocious barking of our dogs. My heart pounded out of my chest as I ran downstairs in a panic, and as I caught glimpses of red and blue lights flashing, I immediately thought, *Brandon.*

October 28th, 2012—The Night of Brandon's Accident

We sat and stared blankly at each other—frozen in our pain—for what felt like hours, even though only a minute or two had passed. I felt the room begin to close in on me, and for the first time in my life, I had to concentrate on breathing. There was a sudden knock on the door, and I can still recall the distinct way it reverberated through my heart.

When I looked up, I saw an officer standing in the doorway. He offered us his sincere condolences and gave us a moment to compose ourselves. He then uttered the words that floored everyone, leaving us all in disbelief.

"The woman who killed your son feels terrible about it," he began. "She is beside herself and is practically inconsolable."

Later, I desperately wished I could have regained my composure long enough to respond right away but instead, his words and the silence that followed still haunt me to this day.

When the unspeakable happens and your world is shaken, it feels nearly impossible to speak or react. Although the officer continued to say a few more words, nothing registered with us. All we could do was stare at him, confused, and hope for an immediate apology for his insensitivity, but one never came. We watched in bewilderment as he made a quick exit until we were finally startled out of our daze when the door slammed shut behind him. Eventually, we would come to learn what his words meant, but it would be years before everything else would fall into place.

A child's death is every parent's worst nightmare, and it is why the officer's words cut even deeper. His insensitivity was our first clue—of many—that would indicate something was not right.

Sharlene Simon was driving home on Innisfil Beach Road from Dave & Busters, a family-friendly sports bar, at around 1:00 a.m. the night she hit and killed Brandon with her Kia Sorrento SUV. Brandon and his friends, Richard Esch and Jake Roberts, were bicycling back home from Tim Hortons, the local coffee shop, when Sharlene plowed into them from behind. She hit Brandon with such force that he was thrown over 350 feet, the impact of his body smashing the front end of her SUV and damaging the roof as he flew backward over the top. Sharlene's police officer husband, Jules Simon, was following behind in his vehicle just before impact.

The boys never knew what hit them.

Brandon's friends were much more fortunate than he was. They had survived the crash but not without significant injury to Richard, who suffered multiple injuries and fractures, including a broken pelvis. Jake luckily escaped the accident without injury since he was riding on the outside shoulder of the road. He was knocked off his bike but evaded direct impact with the SUV.

Unfortunately, Jake could not recall much from that night. He remembered riding late from Tim Horton's and remembered only riding in single file when there was oncoming traffic; otherwise, he stated the three of them rode beside one another. Jake said they didn't hear the SUV coming but remembered Brandon saying, "Oh, shit," right before impact. He said it wasn't until he managed to get up and look around and saw his friends lying lifeless on the road that he realized what had happened.

The boys were not supposed to ride that far out on Innisfil Beach Road that night. Brandon and Jake were hanging out at Randy's house before Richard managed to get a hold of them there, and the three of them, excluding Randy, decided to go out for a quick bite. What started as a ride to Yonge Street for a hot dog at the local gas station, lead to the tragic event a few miles up when they discovered the gas station had closed. They were not being careful and should not have been riding beside one another so late at night, but Innisfil Beach Road is a country road with a speed limit of 80, so cars do not generally fly down it. Both Jake and Richard later attested to having enough time to move when they would hear a car approaching, and both said Sharlene's SUV appeared as though out of nowhere. Randy later recalled having pleaded with his parents to let him go, but they didn't allow it because it was around midnight. In hindsight, Randy was grateful for staying home that night and was profoundly shaken by having come so close to being in that accident.

Melanie, a local Innisfil resident, was one of the key witnesses to the accident and the first on the scene, arriving only mere seconds after it happened. The flicker of the bicycle reflectors in the ditch and the reflection from Brandon's Yamaha jacket caught her eye at first, then, one by one, she saw all three boys scattered on various parts of the road. As a parent, she would later tell me she would not soon forget the sick feeling she experienced at that moment.

Melanie immediately ran to the boys on the road. Richard was still breathing but was badly injured, and Brandon was lying on the road several feet away. Jake had managed to stand up, visibly shaken and unable to speak. She would go on to say that she stayed with the boys until the paramedics arrived minutes later. They assisted Richard as he needed to be transported to Toronto for emergency critical care, but Brandon would not be so lucky.

Melanie held Brandon's hand as he lay on the road with a broken neck before he passed away. She reported that he was not killed on impact but died shortly after. Melanie sat by Brandon's side as he took his last gasping breaths amid police sirens and flashing lights.

The day after the accident, Rick Beasly, the local police chief of South Simcoe, released a carefully constructed letter to the *Innisfil Journal*, the local Innisfil newspaper. The article misinformed the public and stated that Brandon, Richard, and

Jake were irresponsibly biking home from a bush party without wearing helmets or reflective garments and without reflective lights on their bicycles.

Blood from all three boys was taken—without parental consent—including Brandon's, who was already dead at the time. The test results concluded that none of the boys were high or drunk, yet the article implied they were because it reported they were coming home from a local bush party.

Despite the numerous statements made by several witnesses at the scene of the crime about the moon having been bright that night, as well as attesting to the reflective gear on both the bikes and Brandon's Yamaha jacket, the article stated the opposite.

I was so distraught after having read the article that I couldn't sleep that night. I sat up by myself for hours, wondering what I could do. I was furious about the false statements the paper had made and the way the public was led to believe the boys were in the wrong. The article even mentioned the parents, but none of us had spoken to the police nor agreed to the publication. It was frustrating to read the comments made in response to the article and see how cruel people could be. "Maybe the parents should have bought their son some reflectors and a helmet instead of a coffin," read one of the many insensitive comments. It was gut-wrenching.

I immediately consulted Rick Vanderline, the reporter, and he placed another piece in the *Innisfil Journal* and the *Barrie Examiner* that stated the truth. However, it was too late. From social media experience, most people only pay attention to the initial posting about any incident, and even though the follow-up article came shortly after the first, people had inevitably already formed negative opinions about the boys.

Having placed the new article in the local newspapers felt like a small victory, but nothing could have made us feel better at that point. The statements made by the South Simcoe police felt like a deliberate attack against the boys, which was something we couldn't understand. Why would the authorities purposely shed such a negative light on the boys before getting all the facts?

When Derek and I contacted Melanie after the accident, it became increasingly apparent that something was amiss. Sharlene's husband, Jules, did not attend to the boys despite being there before Melanie arrived. Melanie reported that Jules asked her for their location to call 911 but did not identify himself as a police officer or a first responder. Instead, he stood stoically beside Sharlene's car. Neither Melanie nor all three affected families knew that a police officer's wife had hit Brandon for quite some time.

It's hard to believe that a first responder would leave three teenagers lying on the ground at the scene of an accident. I ran over this scenario many times in my head. Jules may have been distraught, but his training should have enabled him to handle the situation. The fact that he did not instinctively run to their aid and instead tended to his uninjured wife spoke volumes. As far as we know, he was never reprimanded or suspended for his actions.

Melanie also reported that Sharlene never got out of the vehicle on her own accord that night, nor was she asked to do so by the South Simcoe police when they arrived on the scene. She was also never required to take a breathalyzer or drug test, despite driving back from a sports bar.

Sharlene's car computer would have recorded her speed at the time of the accident, but it was never taken in for analysis. Moreover, her cell phone was never confiscated, or the records checked.

Initially, the police erroneously reported that Sharlene was doing 90 km per hour in an 80 zone; however, she was never issued a speeding ticket. Down the line, we learned that Sharlene's statement read she had been adjusting her seat warmer at the time of impact and that she had initially thought she had hit an animal. Her heartless comparison cut through us like a knife.

Melanie later told us in confidence that she struggled to understand what had happened that night. She couldn't fathom why she and her husband were required to stay until the early morning hours to corroborate the evidence, while Sharlene and Jules were permitted to promptly leave without so much as a statement. We would later find out that he was permitted to fax his statement weeks after the accident.

I would replay the story over and over again in my head, trying to imagine what had taken place; it was a recurring nightmare that went on for months like a stuck record.

We'd continue to feel unsettled by the events of that night until some months afterward, when all the facts began to surface. We soon discovered that the same officer who came to speak to us at the hospital had been at the scene of the crime.

Brandon's Funeral

Brandon's funeral arrangements were made at the only funeral home in town, Innisfil Funeral Home. Although Brandon had grown up in Mississauga, Innisfil was where he had forged most of his close friendships. We had only been in Innisfil for less than a year, but his visitation was unlike anything I had ever seen before.

As I stood at the front of the receiving line with Derek everything was a blur. Despite my overwhelming sadness, I will never forget the incredible number of people who came to pay their respects that day. People came by the hundreds—friends, family, neighbors—to say goodbye to Brandon. The support was staggering, and I was overwhelmed by the many lives Brandon had touched throughout his short existence.

The day was devastating, to say the least. The feeling of emptiness consumed me, and I felt as though the moment belonged to someone else, as though I was watching everything unfold through another person's perspective. I felt as though I was having an out-of-body experience. I remember looking around the funeral home, trying to connect with someone to get grounded, but all I found was the same look of emptiness in everyone's eyes.

As I gathered up the nerve to look at Brandon lying in his casket, a tangible vulnerability engulfed me; a rushing realization that none of us were truly free from harm, and since Brandon's death, I have never felt entirely safe or unburdened. I strongly believe in listening to one's intuition and gut feelings, and the night of the accident—when I saw Richard's name flash across our call display on the night of Brandon's accident—the apprehension I felt was unmistakable. I would often wonder why I didn't do more to make sure Brandon was safe, but since then, I have learned to never doubt my gut. To this day, I never rode a bike again, nor ever felt at ease when the kids would bike or even walk to school.

When the service at the funeral home ended, we drove to downtown Toronto, where Brandon was laid to rest at a family plot at Parklawn Cemetery to join his grandparents. A young boy buried alongside people who were generations older just wasn't right, and no one could stop crying.

The Trauma of Losing a Child

After the funeral, I knew I would never be the same.

All my life, I had been an anxious person by nature—it was just who I was. I was overprotective and paranoid and was perpetually worried about the kids. Over the years, Derek gently reminded me to let go, stop stressing and learn to relax. It took me a very long time to quiet my nervous system and calm down. I told myself the kids would be okay and that no amount of worrying would change that. Eventually, I learned to break free from my anxiety and embrace a more *laissez-faire* way of being.

Unfortunately, my personal development had come entirely undone the moment the SUV struck Brandon. My previous apprehensions got stuck in my heart once again, and I could no longer sleep for what seemed like an eternity. The anxiety and nervousness I felt within my body and mind were unlike anything I had ever experienced before, and any sense of control I had over my life shattered to pieces, and my paranoia returned with a vengeance.

After the initial shock of the accident, we were thrown into an almost immediate state of disarray, and our life fell apart. Derek succumbed to a deep depression and would not get out of bed, and

I had to urgently shut down my successful daycare business. My house and family were coming undone, and there was absolutely nothing I could do about it. Christopher was only thirteen, and Angelina was only ten, and I had to fight every day to keep myself in check for their sake.

Devon came back home from Toronto and moved into Brandon's room, which was across the hall from Christopher's. I wondered whether it was the right thing for him to do. However, he said he wanted to feel close to Brandon, and sleeping there would help him deal. I was hesitant and couldn't help but think it morbid, but there was nothing I could do. I tried to convince him otherwise, but Devon bottled up his feelings and refused to talk about anything. His behavior was out of character, but at that point, no one was themselves. We were all coping as best we could, trying to carry on in a desperate attempt to appear normal. Every day felt like an uphill battle, and we were all having significant trouble processing what had happened.

Shortly after the accident, the South Simcoe police department called and asked if we wanted to pick up Brandon's bicycle and belongings from the scene of the crash. Derek adamantly did not want to go, so I went instead.

I could not have prepared myself for the heartbreaking consequences of seeing his bicycle, despite believing I had. When I saw Brandon's destroyed bike, it suddenly dawned on me just hard he had been hit. I couldn't imagine bringing the obliterated bicycle home and have it be a constant reminder of his tragic death, so I left it there and only took the clothing he wore that night—his jeans, T-shirt, running shoes, and leather jacket.

In the coming weeks, our insurance company had assigned the entire family grief counselors. In addition, I had also placed the kids in programs at the Seasons Center for Grieving Children, a wonderful organization designed for children who had lost an immediate family member—in most cases, a sibling or parent. The faces of Samantha and Jessica Ramey, aged ten and twelve, graced the upper half of the center's living room/reception area. The two young sisters were killed in a car crash in 1995, and their father founded the organization in their memory the following year. This little place turned out to be a godsend for the kids, as it provided them the chance to be among other children with whom they could create crafts in remembrance of their loved ones and speak openly about their feelings. The counselors encouraged the kids to stare down their grief with a boldness I must admit I lacked at the time. The center also hosted parents in a separate room downstairs, and the sessions were comforting in a way I was not expecting. Typically, I was not one for sharing my deep pain with strangers, but the open environment and support broke down my walls.

Not long after the accident, we received news that Richard's parents were launching a lawsuit against Sharlene. Derek and I discussed it with Venetta and agreed it was not something we wanted to be part of. After all, Brandon was dead, and as horrible as it was, being part of the lawsuit was not going to bring us any closure. We decided against it and put it entirely out of our minds.

Months went by, and nothing changed. I had a household that was falling apart, and I didn't have the mental capacity to look after myself, let alone everyone around me. Deep down, I was terrified that I would never be the same person again. However, I fought to stay afloat.

We had numerous counselors working with us, and all of them advised that only time would heal our wounds. Derek required full-time care as he was marginally suicidal, but I didn't know how to help him. I found myself looking forward to seeing the grief counselors that came to our home weekly, as well as my time at the center with the kids. I welcomed anything that would take me away from the emptiness of the house and potentially equip me with tools to help Derek. Our doctors correspondingly said the same—reiterating that Derek just needed time—though they also believed he needed to be heavily medicated. And hence began the journey of what would be prescription medication overload.

After Derek and I met in 2003, and less than one year after I moved in, Derek started to complain of fatigue and chest pain. After an emergency room visit, the doctor told him that at forty-four, three out of four of his arteries were severely blocked, and he needed an angiogram at once. His family history of hypercholesterolemia required that he take medications for blood pressure and cholesterol, as well as a beta-blocker. His doctor also told him he needed a strict diet overhaul. So, the chicken wings and pizza at midnight had to stop, as did the quantity of beer he drank when he played pool.

Sadly, it was a battle I couldn't win. I was not his mother and never wanted to be, so I would offer my opinion but never told him what to do.

Fast forward to November 2012, after Brandon's accident, when more medication was added to Derek's list of prescriptions. These included Lorazepam and Clonazepam for anxiety and a substantial number of antidepressants to help with sleep and a rapidly developing mood disorder. Derek had so much medication that it was next to impossible to tell whether he was suffering from heart problems or anxiety.

Unfortunately, all the adults in the house were prescribed Clonazepam and Lorazepam for various conditions, mainly anxiety, insomnia, and night terrors for me. I had not slept properly since the night the police woke us up and was therefore grateful to have the pills to help my heart stop pounding out of my chest so that I could sleep.

The way the anxiety gripped my body and mind is indescribable. Of course, the knee-jerk reaction in these situations is to attempt to bring normalcy back to the mind and slow it down, but everyone seemed so far out of control that I felt even more panicked. The counselors repeatedly said to give everyone time to heal, so I prayed for patience and the days of the future when our world would eventually become normal again—or a "new normal."

Prior to Brandon's death, Devon had completed his paralegal certificate and was in the process of applying for a job and looking for a new place to live. He planned to only stay with us for a while after Brandon's death before returning to Toronto. However, months had passed since Brandon died, and Devon showed no interest in going back to the city. He would barely leave the house and was not acting like himself. It was evident that Devon was having trouble dealing with the loss, but he didn't want to talk about it. He buried his anguish deep inside and was undoubtedly starting to drink too much. He was now twenty-three years old, so it was hard for me to tell him what to do, especially when his father had also started drinking in excess. It was a delicate situation to justify to him. However, Devon's drinking was beginning to get so out of hand that I decided it was time for an intervention. I had seen him drink before, but the way it affected him now was different.

Four months after Brandon's passing, Venetta reached out and mentioned wanting to put together a memorial service to commensurate the six-month mark of Brandon's death. I was averse to the idea straightaway. Six months was far too soon for a memorial, and our house was still filled with so much sadness and despair, I couldn't face any more reminders. I worried about what it would do to Derek and the kids so soon after Brandon's death. All I wanted was for my family to try and move on with our lives. Venetta was quick to point out that since Brandon was not my biological son, I could not understand the need to honor and commensurate his loss.

She was right. I did not want to celebrate Brandon's death at all—not at the six-month mark, nor at the twelve-month mark—not ever. I had no issue with celebrating his birthday or hanging an ornament on the tree, or setting a place for him at the table at Christmas—those ideas made sense to me. But reliving his death again only six months later with a memorial seemed awful and unnecessary, and I did not like it. In the end, there was nothing I could do. Both Derek were adamant about having one, so the six-month memorial was going to happen.

Joining the Personal Injury Lawsuit

The anger and emotions ran high in our house at all times. However, the tension seemed to mount when the local townspeople began to fill Derek's head with stories about the night of the accident, and speculation began to grow in his mind rapidly.

We started a memorial page for Brandon and called it *R.I.P Brandon Majewski*. It was an outlet for people's grief where the community, friends, and family could post pictures and share stories. Soon, the heartwarming messages and shared memories came pouring in. However, we did not expect the unforeseen outrage the local community of Innisfil felt toward Sharlene and Jules Simon. In time, the locals began to share known facts about them, which surprised and further angered us.

Initially, only Richard's parents became involved in the personal injury lawsuit at Oatley Vigmond, one of the top personal injury law firms in Canada. Richard suffered critical injuries in the crash and had to be airlifted to Toronto Hospital for treatment. At first, we saw no reason to be involved in the lawsuit, but that all started to change when progressively more people began coming over to the house and calling to talk about what they knew about that night and the person driving the SUV.

Some said the facts now suggested Sharlene was possibly impaired at the time of the accident. However, her sobriety remains a mystery to this day as she was never tested for drugs or alcohol that night, even though she admitted to coming home from a bar and having a couple of drinks.

Sharlene's next-door neighbor also sent us an email saying Sharlene seemed happier than a lark and was going about her business as though nothing had happened since day one.

However, the final straw was when we were informed that the officer who came to see us at the hospital was at the scene of the accident and knew the Simons personally. He was the officer responsible for taking Sharlene away from the crime scene within thirty minutes after she had killed Brandon and injured Richard and Jake. It was then that we realized this was, without a doubt, a case of knowing the right people.

Part of the joys of living in a small town is that news travels fast, and there are always people who know things others don't. However, this was upsetting news and fueled the fire of anger and resentment in our household even more. Almost immediately, Derek decided to join the lawsuit. Derek now desperately wanted his day in court since there seemed to be too many unanswered facts, and he would do anything to get it.

And so, it began.

Angelina's birthday was approaching, and I didn't know what to do. Special occasions had become more stressful than enjoyable. I especially didn't know how to navigate dealing with my daughter's birthday, given my partner had just lost his son not even six months prior. Angelina was now eleven and old enough to understand we wouldn't be celebrating in a big way. I explained that her dad needed more time to heal before being ready for things like sleepovers and kids running around the house again.

She understood, and we planned a small family get-together with some birthday cake instead.

Derek was not ready to celebrate anything yet. He could not bring himself to feel happy. He felt a mixture of emotions—sadness, anger, and confusion. He was sad that Brandon had been tragically killed, angry that Brandon was on the road so late at night, and confused about how the police handled the case surrounding the accident.

The day of Angelina's birthday came, and it was clear it was not easy on Derek. Despite putting on a brave face, Derek was visibly pained.

We set a place for Brandon at the table and placed an 8x10 high school photo of him on the chair. It was beautiful, sad, and awkward all at once, but I felt uneasy as I couldn't tell if it made Derek feel better or worse.

Derek became very emotional and told Angelina this was most likely the first birthday she could remember celebrating without Brandon as he had been part of her life from the time she was two years old. I saw the look come over her young face, and reality hit. At that moment, we all realized Brandon would never have another birthday again. He would forever look just like that high school photo—seventeen years old with tousled blonde hair and big gentle blue eyes.

I wondered if we were ever going to stop hurting and if this hollow feeling was ever going to go away. I didn't blame Derek for how he felt since every celebration was just a reminder of never getting the chance to celebrate Brandon again. I vowed to celebrate these occasions outside the home next time and not torture everyone in this way.

Angelina's little party came to an end as I brought out her birthday cake. It was a beautiful pink and white cake with black stripes like a leopard, with carefully constructed containers of lip gloss made from edible fondant that a friend had made for her. As we sang "Happy Birthday" and watched her blow out the candles,

I noticed Derek put his arm around Devon's shoulders and pull him in close to him, with tears in his eyes. "Don't you ever leave me," I heard Derek whisper to him. His words echoed loudly in my head for the rest of the night.

It was now April 24th, 2013, the day of my birthday. I was feeling sorry for myself for several reasons. I knew in my heart my birthday was not going to be acknowledged, and considering everything that had happened, I didn't expect to celebrate. After all, it was a milestone birthday I wasn't sure I wanted to remember or forget. It was the point that kept getting driven home to me that nothing would be the same again, and I hoped that wasn't true.

The Ghost Bike Memorial

Venetta called to arrange the six-month ghost bike memorial for Brandon. Since we didn't have Brandon's mangled bicycle from the accident, we found another one that resembled the one he rode and painted it white.

The first ghost bike memorial was started in St. Louis, Missouri, in 2003 after a motorist struck a bicyclist in a bike lane. A white-painted bicycle was placed where the accident occurred, with a placard that read: Cyclist Struck Here. Noticing the effect this had on passing motorists, the message caught on, and it became a customary way to honor deceased or severely injured cyclists and serve as a reminder for passing motorists to share the road.

It was May 4th, 2013, and around fifty members of our family and friends gathered at the memorial site on the side of Innisfil Beach Road that day. I had dreaded this day for weeks and prepared myself for the emotional and mental toll it would have on us all.

We hung Brandon's ghost bike on a tree close to the road where the accident had occurred. To the left of Brandon's ghost bike, we hung a blown-up and laminated picture of him taken a month before he died with the words "Beloved Son" written below. We installed a solar-powered spotlight to keep his photo illuminated at night. We also placed a large wooden box in front of the bike for

45

friends and family to place flowers and mementos. People from the neighborhood would always say they were reminded of being close to home when they'd see his memorial on the side of the road.

It was May, but I remember the day being cold and windy. Everything about that day is still a blur—everything but the kids. I remember Derek standing close to the bicycle and making sure everything was hung correctly. I remember holding Christopher and Angelina close as though trying to shield them from what they were experiencing. I hugged them tightly to me, one on each side. Devon stood next to Angelina, and I remember hugging him more than once since he was crying so hard. This was the first time I had seen Devon cry since Brandon died. I had tried to talk to Devon about Brandon's death many times, but it was difficult to get him to share his feelings. I thought it was because he hadn't processed what had happened yet, but today, he seemed changed. I realized then that Devon's paranoia about driving, and his fear of accidents in general, might have played a part in his coming to terms with what happened to Brandon and perhaps created a more profound sense of fear within him. Standing on the side of the road was a pivotal moment for Devon, and he broke down profusely. He was shattered, and I was having a hard time keeping myself together.

I never drove down Innisfil Beach Road at night again for as long as we lived there. If I happened to forget when I was driving, I would turn at 10th Sideroad, a little way's down, so I wouldn't have to pass by Brandon's memorial. Whenever I'd see it, I'd feel sick to my stomach.

After everyone finished laying the flowers, it was time to go back to our house for a gathering. This was the beginning of many memorials, and every year, the plan was to do the same on the anniversary of Brandon's death.

We had a big reception back at the house, similar to a wake with food and drinks. The support from the community was incredibly positive. It was amazing to see just how many people took time out of their day to try to make us feel better. Everyone sat around and reminisced about Brandon, but I wasn't all too comfortable with the attention our family received. I didn't like being taken right back to the day of Brandon's death, but it appeared it was precisely where Derek wanted to be. I tried to understand, but I wasn't sure whether these celebrations were good for us or not. Death and mourning do not come with instructions, and we were doing the best we could under the circumstances, muddling through the dark corners of Brandon's death.

I spent most of the day and evening serving everyone and listening to the conversations from afar, feeling sad and uncomfortable. After everyone left, we sat down in silence for a while and watched TV. I secretly hoped we'd never host a memorial again but never dared to say it out loud. I remember thinking how incredibly selfish I must be to feel that way, but the house felt vacant, as though the life had been sucked out after all the guests had gone home, and I couldn't help but wonder why we did this to ourselves.

Thankfully, I could find some relief in knowing we were leaving for our getaway on Monday. The month before, amid our turmoil and sadness, we agreed we needed a change of scenery and needed to get into a different headspace, and I desperately prayed it would help us find a way back to our old selves.

Later that night, I sent the kids to their rooms to pack their suitcases. Losing a sibling at such a young age had been a struggle for both Christopher and Angelina to process, but I hoped a trip with waterslides and sunshine would offer a miracle cure or help us push the reset button.

The plan was to leave on Monday, May 6th, right after the weekend of Brandon's memorial.

Devon's old friend, Darren, was down from Mississauga that weekend, which was nothing new. Devon had grown up in Mississauga, and Darren had been his neighbor and one of his best friends for years. Darren was twenty-three years old, the same age as Devon, with a short and stocky build and slightly resembled

Matt Damon. Darren had known our family his whole life, so when Devon asked me to pick him up from the train station before Brandon's memorial, I thought nothing of it. However, I reminded Devon we were leaving for Cancun early Monday morning, so Darren would need to leave on Sunday.

Once Christopher and Angelina retreated to their rooms to pack, Devon and Darren went to Devon's room in the basement, and Derek and I continued to watch TV in the living room.

Around midnight, Derek and I, unable to move and too tired to get up and go to bed, continued to watch TV. As I stared blankly at the screen, I suddenly became aware of a shadow lurking in the hallway from the corner of my eye. It was Devon, and he was trying to get Derek's attention. I could tell he had been drinking by the way his body swayed.

"What's wrong?" I asked him.

He ignored me but looked at Derek and said, "You love me, right?"

Derek was exhausted and had drunk quite a lot that night, and Devon's question frustrated him.

"Are you serious right now, Devon? Of course, I love you. You've been drinking too much, and you need to go to bed. We'll talk in the morning," he said, annoyed.

Devon was visibly emotional. He wobbled into the living room and hugged us. I could see he had tears in his eyes, and I could feel his pain, but I didn't know what to do.

Devon left, and Derek went to bed. Before heading upstairs, I went to see what Darren and Devon were doing. It was 1:00 a.m., and they were watching TV and drinking beer. I looked over to Devon's empty suitcase and reminded him he had one day to pack.

"Goodnight, guys. Don't stay up too late," I remember saying, then headed off to bed. I checked in on Christopher and Angelina as I walked down the hallways, turning off the lights. Sleep would feel good; my mind was exhausted, but I felt somewhat lighter thinking about our trip on Monday.

May 5th, 2013—The Unthinkable Happens to Devon

The shaking was relentless and forceful. "Lisa! Lisa! Lisa!" the voice called repeatedly. It felt like a dream, so I didn't wake up right away. "Lisa! Lisa! Lisa!"

I finally opened my eyes and saw Darren standing over me, wild-eyed and frenzied. "I can't get Devon to wake up!"

Still not awake, I asked him what time it was.

"It's almost 7 a.m.!" he screamed. I still didn't understand what was happening. "Lisa, come quickly. Devon's not breathing!"

At that, I was out of bed in seconds and running down the stairs toward Devon's room. Nothing in the world could have ever prepared me for what I saw when I came around the corner. I had never seen a dead person before but instantly knew I was looking at one right then. Devon's handsome face was purple and contorted. He looked tortured, as though he had been gasping for air.

I frantically screamed and instinctively ran out of the house to our neighbors' place and started hammering on the door. Nancy was a nurse, and her husband was a police officer, so I figured they would know if Devon could be saved.

Amid my hysterics, they followed me back to our house, and Nancy immediately started performing CPR on Devon. However, within a minute or two, she looked over at me with tears in her eyes and said there was nothing she could do.

I was stunned. I couldn't move. I heard Nancy call the police but did not register what was happening.

I slowly backed out of the room in a trance and suddenly noticed young Christopher standing behind me. His room was across from Devon's, and my violent screams had woken him up. Christopher had always been a sensitive kid, but I deeply regret not shielding him from seeing his dead brother's body. I immediately pulled him close, and he sobbed into me. I asked Nancy to take Angelina out of the house before she witnessed anything. She ran upstairs, and her husband let me know the police were already on their way.

Once again, I had the horrible job of calling Venetta. I never imagined I would ever have to make this call a second time. I felt sick and took a deep breath before I dialed Venetta's number. Why did I have to do this? Venetta answered on the first ring and sounded frightened. After all, it was very early in the morning.

"Venetta, something has happened," I started.

"What are you talking about, Lisa?" she shouted at me. "Where's Derek?" she asked.

I realized right then that I had no idea where he was; Derek seemed to have vanished. Up until that point, I had only seen Derek once since Darren shook me awake. I remember seeing him standing behind me in the doorway of Devon's room and remember hearing him say, "He's dead."

"I don't know," I finally said. "Just please come to the house. Something terrible has happened, and I don't want to talk about it on the phone. Please come quickly!" I hung up the phone, my heart exploding in my chest. My mind was a battlefield of thoughts, and I couldn't make sense of anything. However, there was someone I could get answers from immediately.

Where the hell was Darren?

I searched the house until I found him hiding in a locked washroom upstairs. I pounded on the door repeatedly until it finally opened. I lunged at him and immediately started shaking him. "What the hell did you give him?" I shouted.

Darren was crying hysterically and shouting at the same time, "He got into my box."

"What the hell are you talking about? What box?" I shook him again.

"I'm sorry, Lisa," he shouted, then wriggled from my grasp and ran down the hall, just as the police and paramedics walked through the front door.

When they saw Devon, they turned and looked at me, giving me a look that said what I already knew. He was dead.

"You already know," they said, and I nodded yes.

I was numb and couldn't even bring myself to cry. I didn't want to be touched, and I didn't want to talk. I felt like I needed to run into the street.

The police questioned Darren and went through his backpack—the same bag he always brought with him when he visited us. They found a lockbox containing a jar of 200 Clonazepam—medication used to control and prevent anxiety—and Tylenol 3s with codeine. Darren told the police he assumed Devon had gone into his box while Darren was asleep and had taken the Clonazepam.

Darren was beside himself and stood motionless as the police continued to question him. In the middle of his interrogation, Venetta came flying through the door in a state of panic, wanting to know what had happened. I told her Devon had overdosed on drugs, and we were in the process of getting answers. At this point, the tears began to stream down my face, and I could hardly get the words out. I had never felt so awful in my life. How could this have happened? The previous night, I had heard Devon and Darren's laughter as I made my way to bed.

The police told us the hospital would perform an autopsy on Devon's body, and we would know what caused his overdose in about six weeks. However, none of this was any consolation because Devon was gone, so what did it matter?

The even more disheartening news was that Darren was free to go with no consequences. The police said that because Devon was an adult and had chosen to take the pills, Darren was not accountable. Venetta was enraged; she wanted justice, but it would not be served.

Derek briefly reappeared to speak with the police, without as much as an explanation of where he had been. He looked mentally deranged; there was no emotion or color in his face. I saw the torment in his eyes after Brandon passed, but I had never seen him look like this before. His eyes were black, dark, and full of pain and rage. There was nothing I could say, but it didn't matter because I couldn't talk anyway as it seemed I was frozen.

Neighbors had gathered outside, wondering what the commotion was about, but I could barely think of talking to anyone, so I hid inside.

Watching the paramedics push Devon out the front door and into the ambulance in a body bag was one of the hardest things I have ever witnessed. My body shook violently from the tears I was trying to hold in. The paramedics awkwardly gave me phone numbers of several crisis hotlines and counseling services and seemed genuinely concerned about leaving us alone. I thanked them, but all I wanted at that moment was for everyone to go so that I could fall apart privately. I was mentally breaking and finding it hard to keep it together.

In his zombie-like state, Derek briefly spoke to Venetta and some family members who had come when they heard the news before asking a friend to take him away. He didn't want to be in the house and left me to deal with everything.

I offered alcohol to whoever was left and sat in silence on the couch. Tears silently streamed down my face as the reality that both Brandon and Devon were dead started to set in. I couldn't face anyone anymore, so I went downstairs to look around Devon's room and be alone.

I replayed the previous night's events in my mind, trying to figure out if there were any clues to what happened. All I could think about was Devon standing in the hallway and asking Derek if he loved him. I remember saying to Derek that he didn't have to respond to Devon that way.

"Devon talks gibberish when he drinks too much; he won't even remember this conversation tomorrow," I remember Derek saying.

Devon's room was a mess as usual, and there were clothes and bottles strewn everywhere. I looked at his bed, and all I saw was his lifeless, purple body and his tortured face. That image would be the source of my nightmares for months to come.

When Brandon died, we chose not to see him in the hospital, given the state his body was found in. The ghastly state in which we found Devon was soul-shattering and shocking, and that look on his face could never be unseen. I would sometimes look at pictures of Devon to remind myself of his handsome face and beautiful warm smile instead of the horrific image that would first come to mind for years afterward.

On the dresser in the far corner of Devon's room sat a half-empty two-liter bottle of Cott orange pop. It jumped out at me like a flashing light, and I instantly heard alarm bells go off in my head. I had read stories about people mixing methadone—medication used to treat severe pain—in orange pop to dilute the bitter taste, but as far as I knew, Devon had never used methadone. However, the police told us there was no evidence of any hard drugs in the house, and all they found were Clonazepam and Tylenol 3s. Devon could have taken multiple Clonazepam, but I felt there had to be more to the story than that.

Strangely, once the police released Darren from questioning and he left the house, he was nowhere to be found. Venetta used to be good friends with Darren's mother and tried to reach out to her with no success. Later, Darren unfriended me and everyone I knew on all social media and would soon become a ghost whom none of us would ever see or hear from him again.

Devon was a beautiful soul and deserved so much better than to be remembered this way. We all want to believe that the world is a safe place and trust that our children will make good decisions because we raised them right. Unfortunately, grief does strange things to people and makes them behave in unimaginable ways. I had a bad feeling about Brandon's memorial taking place so soon after his death, but it was easier on some compared to others.

However, Devon's grief had surfaced that day and overtook his psyche.

Never in a million years would I have ever anticipated Devon's overdose. He was not an angel, but he was not a drug addict either. Unfortunately, we were blind to Devon's suffering because we were still recovering from our individual pain and couldn't see past our anguish. I was so busy trying to keep Derek from drinking himself to death and trying to protect Christopher and Angelina that I didn't pay enough attention to Devon. I couldn't help but see the irony in Devon's death. Devon had always had a phobia of accidents, and I truly believe his overdose was a horrible and unnecessary one.

After a night of zero sleep, tossing and turning, I woke up sweaty and nauseous and feared I would never sleep again. When Brandon was killed, we were often violently scared awake in the middle of the night, and I still had nightmares about him. Would I ever sleep like a normal person again?

Derek and I had barely spoken since Devon was taken away, and I had to force myself to look into his hollow, sad eyes when I addressed him. The jovial, charming, funny, and warm man I fell in love with did not live inside him anymore, and I was worried I would never see him again.

"Don't you ever leave me," he said one day in a loud voice that startled me, with tears running down his face.

"I'm so sorry," was all I could say, overwhelmed and tired. I couldn't stop the tears from flowing. Derek had said those exact same words to Devon only weeks before. In my heart, I knew right then that Derek would never be okay again. How could he possibly be?

Home is the last place we expect terrible things to happen; it is supposed to be the place we feel safe and protected from harm, and it's the outside we are taught to fear. The shock of finding Devon's lifeless body in our own home was too much to endure, and it shook our sense of safety to the core.

For us to accept both Brandon and Devon's deaths would be to admit there is no safe place in this world—something we know to be true but never think about because if we did, we would never let our children out of our sight and we would never sleep at night.

The only way Derek would ever sleep again would be with medication. His nervous system was permanently damaged and on high alert. The empty bottles strewn all over the house every night were far from normal, and constant fear of yet another accidental overdose settled in the far reaches of my mind.

Derek went through the motions and called Venetta to discuss Devon's funeral arrangements, a conversation that Derek could barely comprehend he was having. I could tell by the pained look on his face, that he was slipping into a downward spiral, and I secretly wondered how he would ever function again.

Unlike Brandon, who attended school in Innisfil, Devon did not have many friends in the area. He chose to maintain his friendships with his lifelong friends from Mississauga. Because of this, we decided to arrange Devon's funeral in Mississauga at Turner & Porter funeral home.

I thought planning Brandon's funeral was difficult, as it was, but it did not affect me the way Devon's did. The injustice surrounding Brandon's death was evident. The accident itself caused such commotion and outrage in our small community that the outpour of grief and compassion was overwhelming.

Devon's passing was different; it was derogatory. Devon was an amazing young man with so many qualities worth remembering, but it appeared all anyone cared about was the way he died. No one bothered to remember how his smile could light up a room or how he loved to make people laugh with his sarcastic remarks.

I remembered how wonderful he was and had a hard time fighting back the tears whenever someone asked what happened. I instantly saw a wave of judgment come across their face when I'd say we believed it was an accidental overdose. This was not how I wanted Devon to be remembered, but I was powerless to change it.

I started working on a compelling eulogy for Derek to deliver at Devon's service, describing the bright, positive, and happy guy we all knew him to be. I'm sure these thoughts are what every parent has and deserves to have, but the death of a child leaves one with so many mixed feelings of guilt, sadness, anger, and unfinished emotions that cannot be described in words. It destroys one's faith in the natural order of things and how one perceives the world to be. Most of all, Devon's death made Derek feel a kind of pain from which he would never recover. The blow had come too soon after Brandon's death; we hadn't had the chance to breathe or even come close to healing as a family yet.

Devon's funeral at Turner & Porter turned out to be a small affair, but I was too emotionally drained and numb at the time to care. I couldn't bring myself to contact everyone that I should have, but I could barely think straight, so I left it up to his friends to get the word out. I was overwhelmed and consumed with the fact that he was gone, and the theatrics and services meant nothing to me.

The day felt like a déjà vu, except the faces we saw at Brandon's funeral six months before now looked more confused than somber. I noticed that many people were unable to look us in the eye, but not because they didn't want to, but because they couldn't. They were in disbelief that both boys were dead. Devon's friends were beside themselves as none believed he could have taken his own life. No one knew what to say to any of us, especially to Derek. After all, what could they possibly say?

Many friends and family followed us back to Innisfil immediately after Devon's funeral for a "celebration of life," a term I had been unfamiliar with before now. A celebration of life is a way to pay tribute to a loved one and celebrate their legacy. It is a gathering where family and friends remember the happy times rather than focusing on how their loved one died. At that point, I welcomed the idea of anything that seemed even remotely enlightening.

The celebration of life went over as well as expected, with around fifty to sixty of Devon's friends and family gathered in our backyard to listen to stories told by Venetta and Derek. Christopher and Angelina sat somberly in the backyard, talking to various people and friends. I was afraid how the deaths of both their step-brothers would affect them and knew a lot of counseling was on the horizon for them. I sincerely hoped they would be okay, and in my heart, felt they would be, but it was Derek with whom I was seriously worried. He hadn't stopped drinking since Brandon died.

At one point in the night, a neighbor from a couple of doors down pulled Derek aside and told him that she believed she saw Darren walking at a quick pace at around 6 a.m. on the morning of Devon's death. When Derek told me this, my mind started to race, and all I could think was that Darren must have gone to the beach before he woke me up since Darren had come into our room around 6:45 a.m. My instincts told me he went to the beach to dispose of something in one of the many giant garbage cans. My heart ached indescribably. Darren was nowhere to be found, and once again, we were left with unanswered questions. Not only was Devon gone, but his death was shrouded in mystery and scandal, just like Brandon's.

Why was this happening to us? How could both Devon and Brandon be gone? What would recovery look like, or would it even be possible? My heart wanted to believe it was, but as I looked across the room into Derek's vacant eyes, I wasn't convinced.

Six weeks after Devon's funeral, his autopsy report came in and confirmed my suspicions. The autopsy revealed an excess of morphine in Devon's system and concluded that Devon had overdosed. The bottle of Cott orange pop had been my clue and now proved as evidence, but the source of the morphine was still a mystery and remains to be to this day. With Darren's disappearance and new information about his whereabouts the morning of

Devon's death, we were once again left with unanswered questions and no closure.

Derek had become inconsolable. When Brandon died, Derek curled up in the fetal position and stayed like that for three months, going for days without showering. He was so brokenhearted and sad that the pain would radiate off him so strongly I would feel it whenever I was in the room with him. I felt helpless; all I could do was listen to his tears. However, things were different now. The sick feeling in my stomach was a cross between horror and panic. The dynamic in our relationship no longer made any sense. For the last nine years, there had been six of us, and life had an even flow. How were we supposed to survive as a family with Derek's children gone while mine survived? Life made no sense to either of us anymore, and we had no idea how to navigate our way through the mess of emotions and disparagement.

I no longer recognized the stranger Derek had become. At this point, I couldn't even fathom how I would put things back together again. It was then that I finally realized I needed help, and I could no longer do this on my own; it was time for a family intervention. Part of me wanted to believe that Derek needed the counseling and that the rest of us would be okay. I now knew this was not the case, and it was time we all sought extensive help.

The Intervention

T he grief counselors went into overdrive in a desperate attempt to save our family and try to put it back together again. Our house quickly became a zoo of the comings and goings of different groups of people with different modalities of treatments.

The group of counselors we had onboard knew a severe intervention was needed and worked overtime with us. They believed in the theory that the more we talked and exposed ourselves to the trauma and awfulness of what happened, the less likely we would get stuck in the sadness. As painful as talking about it was, we were told to trust that if we allowed ourselves to feel the pain, it would lift over time.

For Derek, the counseling proved useless. He was still so emotionally broken from Brandon's death that the only emotion he allowed himself to feel was anger over Devon's. He used the family group sessions to push all of us away. He'd yell at us for not understanding his pain and continuously talked about losing the ability to feel. His resentment toward me, Christopher, and Angelina increased with each passing day, and I eventually decided to remove him from our family sessions. He had started to blame the kids for being alive, and their survivor's guilt was slowly mounting. Derek was undoubtedly going to need a lot more time and patience, and no one could reassure me that he was going to be okay. "Give it time," they would say, in the same way people say, "Accept the things you cannot change." I couldn't hear any more positive affirmations from anyone. I wanted to help the kids in their recovery, and Derek was only adding to their anxiety.

In addition to the family sessions, I got private counselors for the kids and received mixed results. Since Christopher was older and on the spectrum, he already had some emotional regulation difficulties. This, combined with his close relationship with Devon, made him take his death very hard. Fortunately, Christopher was assigned a counselor named Nik, who was around Devon's age and, ironically, also looked like him. Nik had a high school teacher's background, as well as experience in trauma and special needs. Christopher was happy with him and stayed in his care for many years after Devon's death.

Angelina, however, was not interested in talk therapy. She told me she felt fine and did not want to participate. I was disappointed and thought she must have been burying how she honestly felt, so I forced her to attend for a while. Her counselor was very accommodating and would even meet her at school for sessions, but Angelina was unfortunately not interested. Out of concern, I had arranged the appropriate psychiatric evaluations for both Angelina and Christopher.

When Angelina and Christopher completed their psychiatric evaluations, I was happy and bewildered to discover that Angelina's tests came back without error. The doctor told me Angelina was a well-adjusted pre-teen and that if she didn't want to participate in counseling sessions, I shouldn't force the issue. The doctor said she, herself, had suffered a loss when she was young and that I should let Angelina cope in her own way. My concern was that it would come back to haunt her later, which it did—the way buried emotions sometimes do. But I wanted to believe the doctor knew best, so I did not question her advice.

On the other hand, it did not come as a surprise that Christopher's phycologist report showed he was suffering from Major Depressive Disorder and an anxiety disorder. Christopher had always been the most sensitive among the kids and tended to internalize his emotions. After Devon's death, however, he began to have uncharacteristic outbursts, and he seemed to sleep all the time.

All at once, my mind was a mess, and I was running on autopilot. I used to care a lot about being happy and positive and used to love to dress up and get my hair done, but that part of me disappeared. I now spent my days running from one room to the next, making sure everyone was okay. Everyone was suffering in their own way, but I had never felt so frazzled in my life and realized I needed help as well. It seemed selfish, but I was so burnt out.

I had already engaged in extensive talk therapy, which helped me deal with Derek's mood swings, but I never discussed the boys' deaths. I was now ready to try just about anything that could provide me with some relief from the suffocation and isolation I was feeling daily.

Over the next few months, I tried several alternative therapies, including meditation, mindfulness, acupuncture, massage therapy, psychotherapy, and eye movement desensitization and reprocessing (EMDR). There was nothing I would not try; I was open to everything offered to me and extremely grateful for all the help I was given. I desperately needed to sleep again and feel well, and I believed in my heart and soul that if I put the work in, one day I would. I extended the invitation to Derek to join, but he was reluctant to try anything.

A few months after Devon's death, Derek told me he needed to get back to work. He was still extremely agitated and upset but believed that being productive again might do him some good, and I agreed. Derek enjoyed his job, but we both knew he was no longer the person he used to be.

Sadly, Derek's return to work was short-lived, and he suffered a mental breakdown in less than a month. He agreed he might have forced himself into work too quickly and decided to return in a month once he had more time to heal. Deep down, he knew that if he had too much time to think about what had happened, he was in danger of losing himself in an even darker depression.

Another month went by, and Derek experienced another unsuccessful attempt to return to work. Once again, Derek took another month off.

In October of 2013, after numerous breakdowns at work, Derek's employer placed him on long-term disability leave. This decision was a blow to Derek's ego, and he did not take it lightly. Willingly choosing not to work was one thing, but being told he was no longer capable was a hard pill for Derek to swallow.

The Year After
Devon's Death – 2014

As unbelievable as it was, we had moved to Innisfil in January of 2012 as a family of six, and only four of us remained in January 2014. In the blink of an eye, our family had become unbalanced. Derek's resentment over my children's survival had become intolerable, and I felt smothered by the negativity in the house. I recall telling my counselors how I had often considered jumping out the window when feeling claustrophobic was too much to handle.

Derek's complicated grief and post-traumatic stress disorder were slowly eating away at him. Derek's triggers for post-traumatic stress were numerous, but he refused to acknowledge them. Much to my dismay, we had stayed in the house where Devon had died. The house was filled with bad memories and ghosts. We had only moved in nine months before Brandon's accident, so there wasn't enough time for us to build any fond memories there. However, Derek wanted to ruminate on the negative memories because that was all he could remember.

Derek would say that every day felt like *Groundhog Day*, referring to the movie starring Bill Murray. Derek couldn't remember or focus on the past dating back before Brandon's death.

For him, every day started and ended the same—waking up and remembering the accident.

The sudden and violent death of Brandon and Devon's unexpected and traumatic death were final and beyond our comprehension and understanding. For a long time, all of us were like zombies wandering through life with no ability to grasp the emotional, mental, and social effects of what was happening to us.

The triggers of memories and reminders were everywhere. This quaint little bungalow that started as a bustling home full of joy now seemed quiet and eerie. At night, the front door would be a reminder of the flashing police lights outside, and when the kitchen phone lit up and rang, it would remind me of Richard's repeated phone calls, not to mention that walking downstairs to say goodnight to Christopher would cause my chest to pound because I couldn't help but look inside Devon's room and visualize his body lying there.

I would silently pray that we would start over again somewhere new, a place where we didn't see Brandon and Devon's faces around every corner and a place where no one knew our sad story or our names. The peaceful little town of Innisfil did not feel like home anymore.

Sometimes, I would stand in Devon's room after he died or sit on his bed, willing him to show himself to me. The spiritual side of me wanted to know if there were such things as ghosts and if Devon could, he would appear. After all, he had died right there in his room.

Derek had raised both Devon and Brandon as non-believers. Devon always spoke of his mother being a non-believer, and Derek had been raised Catholic, but he decided to become a non-believer after experiencing several tragedies throughout his life. He no longer believed in God and would often say that He was cruel if He did exist. Therefore, I always told the boys to think for themselves and not let their parents' ideas or opinions influence their decision to be spiritual. I explained that personal experiences and upbringing shaped their parents' beliefs. Therefore, they needed to search inside themselves for what they believed in and which views gave them peace.

Movies and literature always suggest that when someone passes away, the house they died in becomes haunted. In my heart, I wanted so much for that to be true. The idea of a ghost is not scary if that ghost belongs to someone you love.

I would spend hours just thinking about Devon, anxiously looking for any clue of his presence. One late night, while standing in the kitchen by the window that faced the backyard, I felt a cold gust of wind come from behind me. In that instant, I knew something felt different. The breeze came out of nowhere. There were no vents nearby, but the cold air kept coming, breathing down my neck. At the same time, I felt warm and comforted. Hot tears flowing like lava down my face and in my heart, I hoped it was Devon or Brandon, or perhaps both. I had never felt anything like it before and never felt it again since, but that little sign was what I needed.

It was at this point I began to reflect on Deepak Chopra's *Life after Death*. When I had first read it, I found it interesting on many levels, but the theories never resonated with me until now.

Chopra says there is abundant evidence of "the world beyond" and that death brings us through a door to another level of consciousness. Far more importantly, he states that who you meet in the afterlife and what you experience there will reflect your present beliefs, expectations, and level of awareness.

Many well-meaning family members and friends gave us numerous books, but this one, given to me by our next-door neighbor, stood out to me. My concentration was nil for quite some time, so it took me a while to get around to reading it. However, once I did, my way of thinking changed dramatically, and I wanted to tell everyone what I had learned. I tried to talk to the children about it, but it was apparent it was not something they understood or wanted to discuss. I was never quite sure whether I was supposed to talk to them about Brandon's death. I wanted us to remember him for the funny, crazy things he did and not how he died. But I didn't know the right way to behave in our situation. Do you talk to your kids about death so that they fear it less?

I didn't get to speak to Devon about death before he passed away. We seldom spoke about Brandon's death. I didn't want to cause him added grief by trying to explain my thoughts on the afterlife while he was still processing what happened to Brandon.

Devon was Derek's only biological child left after Brandon's death, so Devon was an emotional sponge for much of Derek's pain and suffering. Devon absorbed it all because he was a sensitive kid, and I could see through his fake smile when we would sit down for one of our late-night chats. We all became good at trying to pretend everything was all right when it wasn't. "Fake it till you make it," right? That's the attitude we put on like a costume along with a smile we use as a mask when life feels unbearable, and we can barely stand to be in our skin. I'm sure every person on Earth has felt like this at some point, but life does not come with instruction manuals. Our family consisted of five unique people dealing with the same tragedy and loss in entirely distinct ways. It was sometimes hard to give everyone the space they needed at different times.

Derek dealt with his grief through feelings of anger and guilt, anger about how the investigation was handled, and guilt around being unable to protect Brandon. He'd play a cruel game with himself and say things like, "If only I hadn't given him money that night," or "If only he had answered his cellphone." There was nothing that could be said to ease or change his frame of mind.

Sadly, the first time Devon and I sat down and honestly talked about Brandon's death was the night of Brandon's six-month memorial. The day was so emotionally draining for Devon that he cried for hours like a little boy when he finally gave into his emotions. We were all so caught up in our various stages of grief, and Devon had been so quiet that I hadn't noticed how much he was suffering. The memorial was much too close to Brandon's funeral and caused a lot of pain for everyone. Unfortunately, Devon overdosed that night, and we never had another chance to talk again.

Christopher was still struggling with a lot of anxiety in response to finding his brother's body downstairs. It haunted him greatly. Christopher looked up to Devon in an adoring way, and his death left a gaping hole inside him. Christopher was only thirteen when Brandon died and fourteen when Devon died. Both tragedies were very traumatic for him, and my heart would break when I thought about how much loss he had to witness firsthand at such a young age. Christopher would always say he felt as though he was stuck in a bad dream from which he couldn't wake. Every night before he'd go to bed, he'd peek inside Brandon and Devon's rooms in disbelief. He couldn't get his mind around the fact that they were gone. Christopher has ADD and high functioning autism, so in conjunction with his condition, the deaths were almost too much for him to handle. The anxiety his grief brought upon him was crippling, and his schoolwork suffered greatly.

Conversely, Angelina chose to bury her feelings and refused to participate in any family therapy sessions. She wanted to pretend their deaths never happened.

As for me, I coped with the tragedies by trying to manage everyone else's grief while trying to remain positive throughout and burying my own feelings.

In March, almost a year after Devon passed away, we decided to take another trip to Mexico in an attempt to bring the family back together again. The negativity and sadness had been so extreme that I just wanted to see the kids smile again. It often felt as though I needed to wear two different faces, one for Derek and his feelings and one for the kids and theirs. It was not always an easy task, and I sometimes wondered whether I'd ever wear a face just for me.

For the most part, our trip to Mexico went well. I'd spend the days with the kids while Derek stayed in the hotel and watched TV, and the family would get together for meals. Derek did his best to enjoy himself, but I know it must have been excruciating for him to go on vacation without his children. By then, I had come to accept that Derek was no longer in control of his emotions, and our situation was as good as it could be at the moment. I was happy that we had a chance to get away, and the kids truly smiled again for the first time in a long time.

The Lawsuit

Whe we returned home from vacation, we all felt much better—a feeling that could only be described as "lighter." The fog lifted, and the change of scenery was beneficial to us all. However, there was something bittersweet about the moment we walked through the door. The last time we attempted to leave on vacation, we found Devon lifeless in bed, and I remember seeing the suitcases by the entryway as the paramedics wheeled him out of the house.

Now that winter break was over and the kids were back in school, life seemed to be somewhat back to normal. I couldn't re-open my daycare yet since we still had several counselors visiting our home weekly, but I hoped to have it up and running eventually.

Christopher and Angelina were doing well in school, and I tried my best to keep up with their counseling. Aside from Derek, the kids and I had begun to respond to the therapy and slowly started adjusting to life. My coping mechanism had been to only speak about the boys' deaths when the kids and I had our one-hour group therapy session or if they ever brought them up with me themselves. My way of coping was in stark contrast to Derek's. He talked about them incessantly and would bring them into almost every conversation.

Derek was still feeling lost and unsure of who he was or what he should do with himself. This internal conflict caused him much frustration, and he began to spend less and less time at home. Derek had struggled with a gambling addiction in his previous marriage, so when I later found out he had started playing blackjack at the casino, it came as no surprise that he had turned to his vice right then. But his self-destruction took the place of who he had been, and I felt helpless to stop him. I worried about our finances but was afraid to approach him because he had become increasingly volatile.

On March 24th, 2014, we received a phone call from Brian, the personal injury lawyer who was looking after the personal injury claim against Sharlene issued by Derek and Richard's parents.

Brian's voice on the other end sounded serious and strained, and I instantly knew something was wrong. Derek put the call on speaker so that I could hear what was being said. "I need you and Lisa to come into the office as soon as you can," Brian started. "Venetta and George also need to come, but I can't tell you the news over the phone. I need to see all of you in person," he continued.

We hung up the phone feeling confused. What could be happening that Brian could not tell us over the phone?

I called Venetta and told her the news, and we made plans to be at Oatley Vigmond the following day. My stomach turned as I wondered what the news could be. That night, I couldn't sleep, and the unpleasant feelings that seemed to have evaporated had once again come back into our house with full force.

The next day, we arrived at the Oatley Vigmond offices early. We were already anxious from the night before but awkwardly made small talk in the waiting room as we waited for Brian to meet us.

Once we were seated in the boardroom, Brain looked around at us and took a deep breath before he spoke, his face pale with seriousness. "The reason I brought you all here is that I have never encountered a case like this, and I needed to tell you in person."

We anticipated his next words and felt stunned as he spoke them, "Sharlene Simon, the driver of the vehicle that killed your son, is suing all of you."

The room fell deathly silent for a moment until everyone began to scream at once, and Derek started yelling in anger. All I could do was watch as I sat paralyzed with shock, listening to his words, with hot tears streaming down my face.

Brian went on to explain that Sharlene launched a lawsuit against all our home insurance policies, our family, Richard's family, Jake's family, and was also trying to include the city of Innisfil for not properly maintaining the roads. She was claiming PTSD and an inability to work, resulting from her despair over hitting and killing our son.

"This is beyond the pale," Brian continued. "In all my decades of practicing law, I have never had a case like this before. This is unheard of, and I am deeply sorry to have to tell you this."

"How? Why?" was all I could manage to say, unable to form proper sentences.

"Unfortunately, there is nothing in the law stopping a person from doing this," he told us. "It's just not something a person would normally do."

I couldn't believe what I was hearing. All I could think was, *what kind of person would do this to a family they had already destroyed?*

The outrage in the room continued around me. Once again, we were struck with a blow so hard that I barely understood what was happening. Our collective devastation was palpable.

I pretended to listen as Brian answered everyone's questions, then heard him say he would be in touch as the case progressed. After we said our goodbyes, Derek and I got into our car and headed straight home in silence. We were mere minutes away from home when Derek, in a sudden hot rage, broke the silence and said, "She's trying to profit from Brandon's death. Does that fucking bitch think she can run over my son and ruin my life and then turn around and turn this into a cash cow for herself? Not a chance in hell! I will kill her myself first!"

When Brandon was killed in 2012, we found out from the locals that Sharlene lived only five minutes from our house on Booth Avenue, and I often wondered whether she might apologize to Derek either in person or by any other means.

However, after a few months, it became apparent that the idea of her reaching out was not likely to happen, and as healing as I thought it might have been, I didn't hate her for not doing so; such a thing would have been incredibly hard and taken a lot of courage.

However, I had never seen the woman and wanted to put a face to Brandon's killer. Derek and I had already wasted countless hours looking for the Simons on the internet but to no avail. It appeared they had no online presence. Coincidentally, Angelina had a friend who lived on Booth Avenue, and ironically, her friend only lived a few doors down from the Simons' house, which had a For Sale sign on the front lawn. More than once, I found myself sitting in the car in front of the house on the street after dropping Angelina off in hopes of catching a glimpse of Sharlene. One time, Angelina came out to ask why I hadn't left. I didn't want to tell her I was waiting for Sharlene to come out, so I pretended I was reading something on my phone.

Who was the woman who took Brandon from us and turned our world upside down?

Three months later, I noticed a Sold sign on the Simons' front lawn when dropping Angelina off and realized I'd have to make my peace with never having seen Sharlene. Ultimately, their leaving provided some form of closure.

None of us ever conceived of the idea that Sharlene had purposely killed our son. We had always believed it was an accident and often wondered what Sharlene must have gone through from the trauma. We empathized with her on some level. However, when we heard she was suing us, our compassion turned to contempt, and I worried about what this would do to our sanity. There is only so much trauma the human brain can handle, and her entitled and reprehensible behavior put Derek over the edge.

There was no coming back from the damage her selfish and heartless actions caused that day. Derek was emotionally shattered already, and this was the catalyst that broke him. Losing Brandon was heartbreaking and Devon traumatic, but Sharlene's cowardice and greed sent our world into a downward spiral.

Derek had slipped into the stronghold of severe mental illness at this point, and I could do nothing but helplessly watch. Who could blame him? He had little time to process one tragedy before the next one struck. Losing his children within six months of each other, followed by a lawsuit, would send anyone into the throes of derangement. He was now battling with a personality disorder, anxiety disorder, and major depressive disorder, along with complicated grief.

Derek was filled with rage and needed an outlet for his pain. I was the closest person to him, so I absorbed most of his emotions— bad and otherwise—and did my best to help. However, I realized there was nothing I could say or do that would ease any of his pain; he was wounded and in a state of disillusionment.

The next few weeks were rough, and I wondered what kind of mother could do this to a family without any regard for their lives or feelings.

I found myself sitting in our silent basement office, sifting through the memorabilia from Brandon and Devon's deaths. I leafed through two binders filled with letters from family and friends and felt the boys briefly come to life. A wave of relief washed over me, flooding me with warm memories as I remembered just how admired and loved they had been.

I knew I had to do something, but what? Our story needed to be heard, but who would listen? I sat down in front of the computer and began writing, "To whom it may concern," and the words just spilled out of me. Tears coursed down my face as I broke my silence and wrote until I noted every detail. To my surprise, I was strangely comforted by the list of horrific events staring back at me from the bright computer screen.

I then looked up the address to the *Toronto Sun*, Toronto's local newspaper, and sent my letter to them, hoping someone would listen. And as it turned out, they did.

The next morning, I woke up on the basement office floor surrounded by papers and pictures, without any recollection of having fallen asleep there. I checked my computer and found an email from Tracy McLaughlin, a reporter from the *Toronto Sun,* asking to meet as soon as possible.

I emailed back right away and told her we would be available all day if she wanted to come by the house. I ran upstairs and immediately told Derek the news and saw his face light up, then turn to confusion as he asked how I managed to get through to someone so quickly. "It's meant to be," I remember saying to him.

Tracy arrived right on time, and when I opened the door to her, I knew I liked her right away. She was small, with a full head of beautiful blonde ringlets and kind eyes. I invited her inside to meet the rest of the family, and she greeted everyone with hugs and tears in her eyes. She told us she had done some research since receiving my email and was deeply sorry for what we had been through.

Tracy wanted to know everything about our story, so we sat down on the couch, and I let Derek speak. I wanted him to recount his version, hoping it would be therapeutic and release some of the tension and fury brewing inside him. I also wanted the public to know what our laws allowed because this could happen to anyone.

Tracy patiently listened as Derek told his story, and I could see tears welling up in her eyes. I sat watching them and felt guilty as I secretly wished our story and life belonged to someone else.

On April 30th, 2014, Tracy's story ran in the *Toronto Sun,* and once again, the support from our community was overwhelming, not to mention the backlash against the Simons. At the time, I hadn't noticed the impact our story had, nor how many people it had affected. I later realized just how connected we all are by our experiences.

The firestorm of media attention that began was far-reaching. The news traveled worldwide, and the outrage was unanimous. I received messages on Facebook from people across the globe, asking what kind of country Canada was for allowing such a lawsuit to happen.

Reporters from France looked for our family on Facebook and found me since neither Derek nor Venetta had accounts. The message I received read: *"Our sincerest condolences for everything your family has endured. It has been more than any family should have to deal with after having lost two children within six short months. What has caused us much confusion and anger is the lawsuit brought upon your family by your son's killer. We have many questions about your justice system. This is unheard of in France."*

The reporters wanted to fly down in two weeks and interview us for a news story that would air in France. I passed the information over to Derek, and he immediately jumped at the chance to talk about the tragedy, and the reporters got their interview.

Shortly after the media storm hit, I opened our front door to a couple of locals—Larry and Laurie—asking to speak with us.

Larry was a local South Simcoe resident with a background in media production who was interested in getting our story out to the public. Laurie was a helpful local mother and a genuinely kind person who had been touched by our tragedies and disheartened by the ensuing lawsuit. They wanted to arrange a local rally against the police and force them to perform another investigation.

Many in the community believed there was favoritism, corruption, collusion, and misleading facts surrounding Brandon's investigation and suspected the story would have played out much differently if Sharlene's husband was not a York Regional Police officer.

We agreed with Larry and Laurie but told them we were too drained to organize anything at that time. They refused to take no for an answer and said they would coordinate it themselves and all we had to do was show up.

Their generosity restored our faith in others, as well as society. It was a much-needed reminder, and it replaced some of the bitterness that had accumulated in our hearts. Larry and Laurie's rally was a godsend for the whole family, as well as a great outlet for many friends who felt betrayed by the Simons' actions. It gave him a place to channel his anger and instilled new hope in getting Brandon's case reopened. We felt confident that we'd finally find some light in the darkness that shrouded the truth.

It had become obvious that Sharlene had been coached on how to sue our family, and in a twist of fate, the opportunity to fight for answers presented itself. Sharlene's lawsuit was beyond distasteful, but what we weren't prepared for was just how far the police would go to protect their own.

Canada / Ontario / News

Teen cyclist struck dead by cop's wife, family's questions 'not answered'

Ian McInroy • QMI Agency

Aug 19, 2014 • Last Updated August 19, 2014 • 2 minute read

Outside police service to review South Simcoe Police investigation into Majewski's death

CTV Barrie

Mike Walker
Reporter/Videographer, CTV News Barrie
🐦 @mikewalkerctv | Contact

Published Wednesday, April 30, 2014 2:34PM EDT
Last Updated Wednesday, April 30, 2014 6:21PM EDT

🚩 Confirmed victory

Justice for Brandon Majewski: Demand an independent review of the police investigation.

TORONTO SUN

Lawyer: Driver suing family over fatal crash was texting

Tracy McLaughlin

Jan 09, 2017 • Last Updated January 10, 2017 • 4 minute read

The Rally

L arry started a petition in April of 2014 addressed to Madeleine Meileur, the Attorney General of Ontario, called Justice for Brandon Majewski. The petition demanded that the Ontario Provincial Police (OPP) conduct an independent review of the South Simcoe police's investigation.

The petition was circulated on the internet and gathered thousands of signatures on Change.org. It stipulated that an outside investigation answers the following questions:

- Why was Sharlene not administered a proper breathalyzer?
- Why was Sharlene's car computer not taken in for analysis?
- Why was Jules following her in his car?
- Why was Sharlene's cell phone not taken at the crime scene and her cell phone records not collected?
- Why were the Simons allowed to leave the scene of the accident right away when other witnesses were required to stay?
- Why were Melanie and her husband's statements excluded from the police report? Was it because they directly contradicted what was indicated in the police report? The police report stated that the road was dark and wet, and the sky was overcast, while Melanie and her husband's

statements noted the road was dry and the moon was bright.

— Why was Jules not required to provide a statement at the time of Brandon's accident? Why was he allowed to send his statement thirty days after the accident?

— Why did Jules, an off-duty York Regional Police Officer, not assist any of the injured boys?

People from across Canada, the U.S.A, the U.K, and Australia signed the petition. Brandon's story and the petition gained a great deal of national and international media attention.

On May 5, 2014, one year and one day after Devon had passed away, the rally took place in the parking lot of the Innisfil Recreation Center, close to where Brandon was killed.

The day was unusually cold for May, and the winds were blustering. It was beautiful to see how many people cared to come together to help our family find some peace in the middle of such turmoil, confusion, and frustration.

Two men playing bagpipes led the procession of family, friends, and community members across the grass before coming to rest in front of a podium in the middle of a parking lot by the Innisfil Community Centre. Derek spoke with tear-filled eyes and a crack in his voice to the assembled crowd. He mentioned Brandon's accomplishments and voiced his regret over Brandon's future as a scientist or inventor. Our family had donated money in Brandon's name to his former elementary school to send a child to science camp, and his corneas were donated to two people after his passing.

Larry spoke to the crowd about the need for justice in Brandon's case. Everyone then watched as the family released black balloons into the sky in honor of Brandon's memory.

A local volunteer filmed the event and passed it to the news media. A report later aired on CTV News, the national news station in Canada, and Simcoe News, the local news station.

The day was beautiful, sad, and draining all at once, but most importantly, it accomplished what it set out to do. Thanks to the local townspeople's support, we were about to get a second investigation into the accident that took Brandon's life and were curious to know what that would look like.

For the first time in years, we were hopeful and ready to finally put Brandon's case to rest, along with the tragic memory of his loss.

Unfortunately, we sadly soon found out the second investigation was nothing like we had expected.

After the rally and petition, the OPP told us they would consider reviewing the South Simcoe police's investigation results, but when it came time to doing so, our request was denied without explanation. Beyond perturbed, we went on the defensive but were unfortunately met with resistance.

In June of 2014, the Toronto Police Service was supposed to investigate the South Simcoe Police Service, but we immediately knew something didn't feel right about one police department interviewing another. The investigation felt like friends interviewing friends, and as we sat in the conference room with the Toronto Police Department, we couldn't help but feel awkward. None of our questions about the officer's or Sharlene and Jules's conduct were answered. The only facts they addressed were the road conditions noted in the police report, which only re-enforced their side of the story that Sharlene was not speeding or intoxicated the night of the accident.

This was the third attempt to get answers to the questions that had been looming since Brandon was killed on October 28th, 2012. Unfortunately, their questions were never answered.

In addition to these attempts, Venetta tried in vain to reach out to the Crown Attorney to get answers. However, nothing came of her efforts, and we were advised to use the services of a civilian oversight agency called the Office of the Independent Police Review Director (OIPRD).

The OIPRD is an independent civilian oversight agency that handles public complaints of police conduct in the province of Ontario within Canada. The party investigates complaints against the police in an arm's length capacity, and none of the employees of the agency are serving officers. Once again, to our disappointment, the OIPRD informed us that the police are allowed a margin of error in their investigations and conduct, and coming from civilians, their ambiguous response was surprising. We knew there was more to the story but were not able to prove anything. At this point, we were becoming thoroughly exhausted, and it had become painfully obvious that our case would remain closed, and there would be no admittance to any wrongdoing. The rally and the support from our community and worldwide attention did nothing to persuade the police to reopen Brandon's case. They kept firm in deflecting our requests and leaving us with unanswered questions.

At this juncture, Derek and I had hit rock bottom. Brandon and Devon's deaths had become our life, and it was all we ever discussed. There was no light in our life anymore, and our family had become divided. In losing Brandon and Devon, I also lost my husband. Derek was still alive but was dead inside. He had now become relentless in making me feel guilty for my children's survival and would often say, "At least your kids are alive."

Christopher and Angelina didn't deserve to feel his resentment, and I was exhausted from feeling torn between both relationships. I knew in my heart that things weren't right and that I needed to make a change; however, the more I thought about leaving, the more I stressed myself out. I'd lay awake at night wondering what kind of person could ever leave someone who was struggling as much as Derek was. However, I couldn't do it despite fighting to breathe as the burden and weight of our tragedy strangled me.

Over the next few months, my Facebook messenger box continued to overflow with messages and condolences from numerous strangers. Their continued support truly touched my heart.

Since the boys' deaths, Venetta and I had been in contact regularly, and we came together for the sake of our families. So, whenever I would get new messages, I would copy and send them to her. I wanted her to at least feel some joy in the beautiful things strangers were saying as I knew she was suffering intensely. Amazingly, any unsettling feelings I had harbored about the boys mother when the boys were alive had long disappeared, and she and I had ironically become bonded in tragedy.

It was early 2015 when I opened my Facebook, and my mouth dropped. I received a message from a local Barrie real estate agent named Mandy. The beginning of her message read, *"I have been contemplating contacting your family for a long time now. I have information about the night your son was killed that I think you should hear. I have struggled between keeping this information to myself and sharing it with your family. But the truth is, not telling you is eating me up inside, and being a mother, I know your family deserves to know the truth."*

My heart raced in anticipation of what was coming next. *"Sharlene was a friend of mine, and while I was driving with some friends one day, she confessed over Bluetooth that she was texting her mother at the time she hit and killed your son."*

I couldn't believe what I was reading. My heart was pounding so loudly that I could hear it, and the tears were flowing so fast that I couldn't see the computer screen anymore. This was what we had always suspected, and now, I was reading the proof. I couldn't believe it and could barely wait to tell everyone. I was overwhelmed with gratitude.

I quickly wrote her back and thanked her from the bottom of my heart for deciding to come forward. Mandy was quick to tell me that she had a family of her own, and she did not want to be on anyone's "radar," and I immediately understood her need for privacy.

We sent a couple of messages back and forth, and she admitted to being disgusted that someone she knew and trusted could conceive of doing something like this out of greed.

I finally worked up the nerve to ask her what I had been waiting to ask all along. I wondered if she would be willing to talk to our lawyer to prove Sharlene had lied. Up until this point, we had been banging our heads against the wall, hoping to get the truth.

However, when I pressed send and my message delivered, her messages stopped, and the screen went blank. Mandy had logged off. I waited for a few minutes but soon realized her lack of response meant she was uncomfortable with my question. I knew it was best to let it go right then but prayed she would recognize how much we needed her help.

It's incredible how one small and courageous move by a single person can have the power to change everything.

Up until this point, we were led to believe that Sharlene was playing with her seat warmer, and she had claimed she thought she had hit an animal. Those hurtful words came up in conversation more often than I wanted to remember. What Mandy told me was a hard pill to swallow, but her narrative changed everything, and the story was finally making sense. I just hoped it wasn't too late.

I dialed Venetta immediately as I could barely contain myself, and I could hear the tears in her voice on the other line as I spoke. She and Derek had already suffered so much, and this was a life-changing moment for us all. Mandy's information was the start of a turn of events that would change the course of our lives, and I wondered whether Mandy understood the importance of her input.

It suddenly felt like someone had thrown water on me and had woken me up again. I immediately started pouring through my inbox, carefully looking for more answers, when I came across another intriguing email from a local woman named Laura. She wrote saying she had been friends with the Simons for years and wanted to share some background information about them that might help us. I decided to meet Laura. I needed to know and find out as much as possible. Up until now, we knew nothing about the Simons—not even what Sharlene looked like.

Laura and I met at her home in Innisfil. I was both apprehensive and excited at the same time. I was nervous about meeting anyone who said they were friends with the Simons. After all, as far as I was concerned, they were the enemy, and I had no reason to trust anyone anymore.

The second Laura answered the door, I felt relieved. She smiled at me warmly, invited me into her home, and showed me around. I quickly learned she had lived there for years, made a living as a local business owner, and had also worked outside the home as a counselor. She told me she had known Sharlene's mother, Donna, for decades and said that Donna had launched multiple lawsuits over the years, looking for a payout. Laura mentioned that Sharlene's behavior did not surprise her, given their family's history.

Laura had prepared for my visit. She had laid out photos of Sharlene that I could take home with me to show everyone. Up until now, the mystery of Brandon's killer's face was something we had to accept. But here it was now, right in front of me. Sharlene Simon was no longer the woman without a face.

Laura also showed me Sharlene's kids through her mother, Donna's, Facebook. As I looked at photos of her three beautiful and healthy kids, the reality of the lawsuit sunk in. Sharlene's "cash grab" extended to claiming money not only for her PTSD but for her husband and children as well.

Laura explained that Sharlene had been a former adult entertainer until she met Jules. She added that she had worked at "Solid Gold," a strip club in Burlington, Ontario, and her stage name had been "Desiree." None of this was relevant to our case because an individual's character makes no difference in a court of law. However, it was information we were hungry to know since we had received minimal facts about the Simons.

Much like everyone else, Laura was devastated to learn about the lawsuit against our family. Everyone knows what it feels like to have salt rubbed into wounds. Nonetheless, when salt is rubbed into the wounds of parents of a dead child, parents everywhere relate in a universally empathetic way.

I thanked Laura for reaching out to our family with a hug, a smile, and a goodbye. I told her that light was slowly starting to shine on our story in a way it hadn't before, and I was forever grateful for her assistance and support. As she closed the front door and waved goodbye, I walked to my car, my arms full of papers and photos, and could feel a sense of relief wash over me. I looked around and suddenly realized what a gorgeous little town we inhabited. The sun was shining, and trees lined the streets as far as the eye could see. Sunflower fields rolled past the roads, and there were horses in several of our neighbors' yards. But, the most beautiful part about it that I had failed to notice over the past few years was just how peaceful it was.

The first thing I did when I got into my car was called our lawyer. I was excited to tell him what Laura had shared. I felt a sense of satisfaction and accomplishment; the puzzle pieces of our story were slowly starting to make some sense, although we still had a long way to go.

When Brian answered the phone, and I gave him all the details, to my annoyance, he told me the information about Sharlene had no bearing on our case. My heart sank, but the more I thought about it, the more I realized it was true. I just wanted something to happen that would change things and shed some light on the darkness. Even if I verified the information to be true, it wouldn't make any difference; a person's character is not relevant in determining guilt. Brian told me to be patient and said an engineering firm was going to conduct an accident reconstruction report over the next couple of months that would provide substantial evidence for our case. However, I couldn't bring myself to care at that point. I wasn't sure I could handle any more potential disappointments.

Brian's response was beyond disappointing, and I wanted to put an end to the litigation despite having learned more in the last couple of months than we had in the previous three years. Back then, we were told we would have our day in court, and Sharlene would have to answer for all her actions. I had told Derek that none of us were ever going to heal with a lawsuit hanging over our heads, but when damming information began to leak, we had no choice but to fight to get our questions answered.

To add insult to injury, our lawsuit was set to go before the courts in early 2016. Unfortunately, due to Sharlene filing her counter-suit against all our house insurance policies in 2014, another two years were added to our court date. It was now pushed into early 2018—five long years of torture.

Having another two years added to the "jail sentence" was unthinkable to me, and I began to wonder why Derek wanted to prolong their agony and suffering. The family needed to heal, and this lawsuit was slowly suffocating us.

—◦◦◦)◦(◦◦◦—

It was now the summer of 2016, and I had finally had enough. I was thoroughly drained, trying to keep a man happy who now ignored everyone and substituted TV, alcohol, and gambling for human relationships. I could not reach him anymore and had given up trying. I realized that the Derek I knew and loved was gone. His survivor's guilt had completely taken over his personality, and I could no longer reach my partner. I had become a single parent, completely isolated in her own home.

This was a terrifying thought, but with my grief and family counselors' help, I decided to confront Derek and give him an ultimatum. When we care about someone, we can't stand idly by and let them continue down a self-destructive path. At some point, we need to step in and do something—for their benefit and ours.

I told Derek I had been looking at treatment centers in Guelph, Ontario, and found one specializing in mental health and addiction treatment called Homewood Health Center. At first, I was met with anger and defiance. Derek repeatedly said he didn't need treatment; all he needed was time. It was the response I had expected because he was comfortable on the path he was on, but I was desperately unhappy, and so were the kids.

I continued calmly and explained to him that his behavior was abusive, and it was negatively affecting everyone in the house. I told him he was slowly killing himself with his drinking and excessive eating. He had gained sixty pounds in two years, and his face was always red from drinking and elevated blood pressure. I told him I couldn't stand by and watch anymore.

In the past, I had subtly begged and pleaded with him, but it had gotten me nowhere, so this time, I knew something had to change. We could no longer continue living this way. He either attended a treatment center, or we would have to go our separate ways.

He looked at me with tears in his eyes, realizing I wasn't taking no for an answer. I was not ready to give up on our family yet. My last hope was that intense therapy and being forced to give up all substances would be the help he needed. I wanted the best for him, and I wanted him to heal. I didn't want him to live the rest of his life this way. And he finally agreed.

I sent a text to our grief counselor right away, excited that Derek had agreed to a full-time in-patient treatment program for post-traumatic stress disorder and substance abuse. Our grief counselor texted back almost instantly and said he'd get Derek on the waiting list at Homewood Health Center.

Derek's admission date was quickly set to November 28th, 2016, a couple of days after Christopher's birthday. Derek's admission date was still almost three months away as we were at the end of August, but I was glad we had a solid date. It was a positive sign as far as I was concerned.

A few days later, after having taken the kids shopping for back-to-school clothes, I noticed a message on Facebook. It was from Mandy, the real estate agent who had messaged me several months earlier. Excitement mixed with anxiousness stirred within me as I secretly hoped she had reconsidered talking to our lawyer.

Her message read: *"Dear Lisa, I want to let you know I have thought about our conversation and have talked it over with my husband. He and I both agree that helping your family in any way we can is the right thing to do. I am prepared to give an affidavit, stating that I, along with several others, heard Sharlene admit to texting her mother when she hit and killed your son. If need be, I will also testify in court to re-enforce my statement. Please provide me with your lawyer's contact details."*

I messaged Mandy back, thanking her for the selflessness and compassion she had shown our family. I told her that her testimony would give us the strength to believe in our case once again, and we were grateful to her.

I received a phone call the next day from Brian telling me that Mandy had signed an affidavit, saying Sharlene had confessed to her that she was texting at the time of the accident, contrary to her statement stating she was playing with her seat warmer and thought she had hit an animal.

The details were finally starting to make sense. I now had hope that we could win our case, which, strangely enough, was not something I could have cared less about when this all started in 2013. At that time, all I wanted was to be left alone and was furious that we had gotten involved in a lawsuit surrounding Brandon's death, but that all changed when Sharlene launched the lawsuit against us. Her callous act changed something inside me, and a rage I didn't even know existed formed.

The lies were now starting to make sense as others helped us fill in the blanks. Karma seemed to finally step in when we received news from the reconstruction report on top of the affidavit. The report proved that Sharlene was driving between 103-117 km per hour at the time of the initial impact, evidence that was in stark contrast to the 90 km per hour noted in Sharlene's statement. This evidence would help explain why Brandon was thrown over 350 feet, including the extent of both Brandon and Richard's injuries. The speed at which she was driving and the fact that she was texting was more than enough evidence to prove this accident could have been avoided. I was beginning to see there was a reason to fight in court after all. I wanted the world to know Sharlene was speeding and texting and that there would be justice in releasing that information to the public. Finally, there was nothing to stop us, and Derek would have his winning day in court.

The news lifted Derek's spirits, and he finally agreed to a new start outside Innisfil and away from the house that had been haunting us for so long. We quickly made plans to move before his twelve-week program at Homewood Health Center started and found a beautiful home with a large backyard and swimming pool in Horseshoe Valley, Ontario, away from our tragic past. Life was finally starting for us again, and I was hopeful for the future.

Doctor Visit Before Rehab

Derek had been complaining about back pain throughout the summer and had spoken to his doctor, Dr. Maharajah, multiple times about it. However, Dr. Maharajah had attributed his back pain to extreme stress and tension, as well as complicated grief and PTSD. Derek was advised to go for massage therapy weekly and physiotherapy bi-weekly to break down the tension in his shoulders and neck and try to lose some weight.

I had noticed the swelling in Derek's shoulders and neck, and at first, chalked it up to his sudden weight gain.

Derek had been seeing Dr. Maharajah regularly since the day Brandon died. He saw him for weekly half-hour counseling sessions, then continued to see him even more frequently after Devon passed away six months later. His visits were numerous, and I've never seen anyone spend more time in the doctor's office than Derek. Dr. Maharajah would check Derek's blood regularly and was always there as a support system when Derek needed it. He went above and beyond regular protocol and made it his full-time job to help rehabilitate Derek.

However, despite all the monitoring, psychological treatment, and testing, I saw very little positive change in his mental or physical health in the last three years. If anything, the complete opposite was true.

In June of that year, I had asked Derek to get a second opinion regarding his back pain, but he was not interested. His faith in Dr. Maharajah went beyond one's regular trust in one's doctor. Dr. Maharajah was Derek's elementary school friend, and he trusted his judgment and viewpoint above all others.

Occasionally, I'd go to the appointments with Derek and would ask questions about his mental health. However, it seemed as though no one ever listened when I tried to explain Derek's suffering to them. I had repeatedly told Dr. Maharajah that if Derek didn't get help for his mental health, his sickness would manifest physically. Nevertheless, survival was an effort for Derek at this point, so all I could do was wait for his upcoming admission to Homewood Health Center. I saw it as his last chance to pull his mind back together, and I was hopeful. We have nothing if we don't have hope and are not open to the possibilities that change can bring.

On November 24th, 2016, four days before his admission to the Homewood Health Center, Derek left for Mississauga early in the morning to see Dr. Maharajah for a last-minute appointment. Because physical activity was going to be a major part of the rehabilitation program at the Homewood Health Center, Derek decided to get an MRI to ensure he could participate. Dr. Maharajah had completed the MRI a week prior, and Derek was on his way to get the results.

A few hours later, I still hadn't heard from Derek, which was highly unusual as he would typically call me the moment he'd leave his doctor's appointments. I sent him a text asking how it went and waited for a reply. Another hour passed without a response. I was beginning to panic, so I called him, but he didn't pick up. I called again. After a few minutes of pacing around the house, Derek finally called while I was in the bathroom.

"Hello, is everything okay?" I asked him slowly. The phone went silent. "Hello?" I repeated.

When he started to speak, I immediately knew something was wrong. His voice was shaky, and I could tell he was upset. "No, Lisa, everything is not okay. I have cancer."

I could hear him begin to sob on the other line as I screamed, "What? Oh, my God!" I instantly dropped the phone on the bathroom floor and fell to my knees, unable to believe what I was hearing. I locked the bathroom door and screamed.

After an indefinite amount of time, I picked myself up off the floor and pulled myself together. I understood that my brain responded differently to stress after the trauma of Brandon and Devon's deaths. Now, whenever I sensed fear, every circuit in my body fired at once until I felt utterly exhausted. I would then calm down and feel nothing until I recovered my strength. I now identified these familiar sensations and knew something was wrong, but I didn't want to believe it. Not again. We had already been through so much.

The kids were home but still asleep, and I didn't want them to see me like this. After all, I didn't have the full story yet, and I might have been overreacting. My optimism was what had gotten me through everything thus far, so I told myself to be strong. There wasn't anything that life had thrown at us that we couldn't survive, and right now, Derek needed me to be positive. I decided to put a smile on my face and calm down.

I watched out the living room window as Derek's black Mercedes pulled in the driveway, and I practiced fake smiling a few times before he walked through the front door. I honestly couldn't even feel my face; I was so shaken that I felt nothing inside my body. As soon as he walked in the door, his face told me everything. He looked tense, and I could tell he had been crying. He looked like a man ultimately defeated, an altogether different man than the one who left the house that morning.

The Diagnosis

You can tell a lot from a person's eyes, and I had been watching the love and life leave Derek's for a long time now. I didn't blame him. What happened was not his fault, and he had been emotionally struggling now for years. He stared at me blankly, without saying hello, as he handed me three sheets of paper.

I sat down on the step leading into the living room and immediately started to read the pages. They consisted of an MRI, a bone scan, and a summary. I had never looked at anything like this before, but I didn't need to be a doctor to know the pictures were bad. His entire skeletal region from the shoulders down to the spine and pelvis showed black against the white paper. I couldn't blink as my eyes started to fill with tears. The translation from the radiologist read: *"Widespread osteoblastic bone metastases."* Further down, it read: *"The features are those of metastatic adenocarcinoma."* I could no longer hold in my fear and hugged him as I had no idea what to do or say.

After an emotional last visit to Dr. Majarajah's office, we were released from his care and referred to an oncologist at Trillium Health Centre in Mississauga. Dr. Majarajah explained that Derek had the misfortune of being a non-secretor of the prostate-specific antigen (PSA), and apologized for not having detected the disease sooner, despite Derek's regular blood testing.

The very first visit with the oncologist said it all. The doctor walked in the room as though he had done it a thousand times that day already. He was a very tall and thin older man with glasses, a head full of thick white hair, and what looked to be a permanent grim look on his face.

"My name is Dr. Gapski, and I will be your oncologist, Mr. Majewski."

I was surprised at his age as my eyes scanned the tiny hospital room we were sitting in. I felt nervous and nauseous in his presence, and my mind raced. I couldn't help but wonder how many people he gave fateful news to every day. If the look on his face suggested anything at all, it was making me feel very nervous and uncomfortable.

He barely looked up at us as he scanned the computer and read Derek's file.

"Has your doctor gone over the results of your recent scans with you?" he asked grimly. Derek told him he had and that his doctor needed an oncologist to diagnose the scans accurately.

"I'm going to be honest with you, Mr. Majewski. The news is not good. The cancer has spread from its original site, which I am almost sure is the prostate. It has spread extensively throughout your bones, affecting mainly your spine, shoulder, neck, and pelvic area."

At this point, I could not contain myself any longer and asked, "What does this all mean? What kind of treatment will he receive? Is he going to be okay? Can he still attend Homewood?" The questions spilled out of me, and I was overwhelmed beyond belief.

He took a deep breath and looked up at me, "I am going to be as direct and honest with you as I possibly can, Lisa. The news is not good. I would not suggest that Derek attend Homewood at this time. He will need to begin cancer treatment immediately to minimize his pain. It is only going to get much worse."

I could barely swallow as I heard his words. I knew we were there because he had been diagnosed with cancer, but I was not mentally equipped to hear what he had to say. "What did you say?" I blurted out absentmindedly.

"What I'm trying to say is that Derek's cancer has spread way out beyond the site and into a vast amount of his bones. For lack of better wording, this type of cancer is not treatable. Based on the scans, I estimate that Derek has roughly six months to live. I am so very sorry to have to give you this news," he said, then added, "I will give you a moment alone."

The room went dead silent, and strangely, I did not cry. I just sat there and felt completely numb. I knew the feeling all too well as I had felt it after Brandon and Devon's deaths. However, I experienced it much longer after Devon passed, but this was different.

I avoided looking at Derek for a moment. I couldn't bear to see the pain I knew would be staring back at me. As though in a trance, I stood up and hugged him as he continued to sit. We had suffered so much, and at this point, life almost didn't feel real anymore. It had become a living nightmare.

I could feel my left shoulder getting hot and wet, and Derek looked up at me with eyes that surprisingly had life in them. I had not seen any real emotion in them since Devon died.

However, the man looking back at me now had a different look on his face; he almost looked human again.

This was the moment I remember, the moment Derek decided he no longer wanted to die. He wanted to fight for his life, and just like that, I saw a glimpse of the man I used to know.

Dr. Gapski returned to the room a few minutes later with an option for Derek to consider. Even though his condition was not treatable, a STAMPEDE trial was available for his type of cancer. A STAMPEDE trial is a systemic therapy in advancing or metastatic cancer for the evaluation of drug efficiency, and the doctor said it could buy Derek an extra eighteen months. The downside was that it would involve nonstop treatments. On top of the hormone therapy and bone treatments that were already scheduled, he would be receiving a series of radiation treatments, followed by chemotherapy.

We now needed to review a new set of papers stipulating Derek's treatment schedule. At the time, neither of us understood that by agreeing to the STAMPEDE trial, Derek was buying himself an extra eighteen months of intense pain and suffering spent mostly in hospitals and various clinics around the city.

Leaving the oncology ward that day was a sobering experience for me. I looked around at everyone in the hallway as we made the long walk back to the elevators. I saw so many faces full of sadness and despair and many patients with wigs and scarves wrapped around their heads, looking cold and frail. I tried to smile at as many of them as I could, wrapping my head around the fact that the waiting rooms were full of cancer patients daily.

Until that day, I had never been in an oncology department, but it dramatically changed my life. It was a forceful reminder that life is fleeting, and if it can happen to others, it can also happen to us.

After Derek's meeting with the oncologist, life turned into a flurry of appointments at local hospitals in the Greater Toronto Area, and they did not end there. We also made trips to the University of California, San Francisco, for consultations to determine whether Derek was a candidate for immunotherapy, and his records were sent electronically to The Mayo Clinic in Minnesota and John Hopkins Hospital in Baltimore.

Despite desperately holding on, there was nothing we could do. The results from all the top cancer hospitals drew the same conclusions. The cancer was too widespread, and there was nothing left to do but minimize Derek's pain.

I spent a couple of months furiously searching the internet, trying to find another answer, unwilling to accept Derek's death sentence. Ultimately, I realized that everything the doctors told us was true. It was time to enjoy what little time Derek had left. And he did.

Derek spent most of his days heavily medicated on medical marijuana mixed with various prescription painkillers, including OxyContin, Percocet, Morphine, and Methadone, when all the others stopped working. He was extremely happy and positive. It was as though he had accepted his fate and was grateful he could choose how others would remember him. Not unlike Brandon and Devon, who were ripped from our lives without warning or the chance to say goodbye.

As far as he was concerned, it was his funeral, and he was going to live life while he still could. He proceeded to purchase a Ferrari and gave our 34-foot boat to his nephew because he bought a 50-foot Carver. I questioned whether he should be driving anything anymore in his medicated condition, especially a Ferrari.

I tried to voice my concerns about Derek's impaired driving to his palliative pain management doctor, Dr. Shama. When I delicately brought it up, Derek became hostile. I tried to see things from his perspective; if I were in his shoes, I wouldn't want anything else stripped from me. But, given how Brandon died, I wanted him to realize that he could hurt someone.

The doctor seemed unfazed by my concern and said the drugs Derek was on do not impair a person's ability to drive when used correctly. I wanted to argue, but I didn't. Once we left the room, I felt guilty for not telling the doctor that Derek was also drinking and smoking marijuana.

I was halfway down the hall when she called me back into her office and asked if she could speak to me privately. She could feel I was upset and to appease me, said that due to the rate at which his cancer was spreading and how much pain he was in, Derek wouldn't be driving for much longer. I nodded in response and closed the door without saying much else.

After this visit, Derek's health deteriorated significantly, and it was only a month or so before he could no longer drive. The cancer had spread throughout his entire spine, and he could no longer sit properly. He spent most of his last summer sleeping on his new boat and playing Blackjack at the casino. It was one of the few things he could still do, so even though he was in a wheelchair permanently, I would take him to play, and he was grateful that I'd wait for him for hours.

Eventually, the drugs or cancer—or both—took their toll, and he no longer had the mental dexterity to add cards correctly, and he started to lose consistently. It had become increasingly evident that the pain was becoming more and more challenging to manage, and despite copious amounts of drugs, this was a sign that something had changed.

In the end, Brandon's case would not make it to trial. The case was mediated out of court due to Derek's terminal illness. Derek regrettably never got the justice he so desperately wanted. Sadly, to this day, we still don't know why Sharlene could leave the scene of the accident within thirty minutes of killing Brandon, nor why her cell phone records and black box from her vehicle were never taken in for analysis. There was also the question of why she was not given a proper breathalyzer test when blood was taken from all three boys, including Brandon's dead body, without our permission. None of our questions were addressed, and we were forced to accept the result and finally move on.

Derek's Last Birthday and Living Funeral Combined

It was now June of 2017, and Derek had been diagnosed on November 26, 2015, almost eighteen months to the day. He was deteriorating quickly, so I planned a "living funeral" for his 57th birthday.

I invited everyone we knew and ordered the biggest pig I could find from a local company that delivered it and set everything up for the roast. I also enlisted the help of everyone I could to help get the day organized.

A massive tent was set up in the yard, and there were hundreds of people wandering around. Devon and Brandon's friends pitched their tents across the lawn, and our backyard resembled a small Woodstock. It was both a heartwarming and heartbreaking day. It was painful to see everyone from Brandon and Devon's funerals mixed with Derek's friends who had come to pay their respects. Many arrived who Derek hadn't seen in years. Since he had become very reclusive over the past few years, most had not even known he was dying of cancer.

I attempted to make the best of the day by drinking a lot more than usual. I walked around smiling at everyone, trying to make the best of what everyone knew would be his last birthday. However, had I not known the circumstances, I would have said it was a fantastic party. This was my first living funeral but not the only memorial I had hosted in recent years, unfortunately.

Derek still looked healthy. Surprisingly, he hadn't lost any weight yet, and his face still had color and life in it. If I didn't know any better, I would not have known he was ill.

When his birthday cake was brought out into the backyard, and everyone began to sing "Happy Birthday," Derek dove off the diving board into the pool. Even though the inside of his body was entirely ravaged, he resurfaced with a giant smile on his face. He later told me that the plunge hurt his body tremendously, but he was happy he did it. He wanted his friends to always remember that moment.

I was grateful for having hosted the living funeral when I did because the next six months were a steady downward spiral. The hormone treatments had stopped working, and Derek only had a couple of chemotherapy treatments left. The oncologist described Derek's cancer as "active as a teenager running circles." The disease was vigorous, dynamic, and out of control.

I could not have handled Derek's last few months without the help and support of my friends Christine and Steven from Hamilton. They were my rock during what could only be described as a torturous process. They would show up whenever they had the chance and selflessly gave their time and energy. I will forever be grateful to them for their unconditional love.

I was also grateful that our time in the chemotherapy ward was coming to an end. It was the absolute saddest place on Earth. My heart would break, and I'd get short of breath when I'd make eye contact with the other patients. I would feel their pain, and it would hurt my soul. However, I would bury my sadness and instead give them a big smile.

Watching the staff in the oncology department at Trillium Health Center made me realize that it took an extraordinary type of person to work with cancer patients, and I often wondered how they managed.

It seemed that the treatment was worse than the disease. Derek would leave the ward exhausted and nauseous, unable to eat and barely able to drink. The weight began to fall off his body, and he no longer enjoyed eating. I continued with my regimen of juicing carrots and beets, but he barely drank any of it. His diet mainly consisted of pain medication, medical marijuana, and Ondansetron—medication to control his nausea. The only thing he could eat was white chocolate macadamia nut cookies and Tim Horton's coffee. This combination eventually became his daily meal until the end.

In reality, I lost my husband in 2012, after Brandon death, and following Devon's fatal overdose, he became emotionally gutted, and we grew apart even more. I lost all hope after the lawsuit was launched against us in 2015 and his subsequent cancer diagnosis. At that point, through a painful twist of fate, we lost whatever was left of our physical relationship. We had struggled to find normalcy since Brandon's death, but it just never seemed to be in the cards.

What little life he had left was stolen from him by the anti-androgen hormone treatments. The treatments were meant to slow down the spread of the disease by blocking testosterone production and depriving the cancer cells. Derek's condition devastated him, and the hormone treatments made him cry endlessly, wondering what was left for him in life. I could say or do nothing that would make him feel any better, so I would just give him my time and make sure he was looked after and was comfortable.

He had wanted to travel to Jamaica when he first became sick, so we managed to take the trip. I spent much of it alone. I couldn't enjoy myself knowing he was sleeping and overheating in the hotel room. He couldn't move or do anything. It was too painful for him. That was the last trip we took together.

Derek had a bucket list and checked most of the things he wanted to do off. He bought the boat and Ferrari and enjoyed them until he couldn't anymore. He wanted to see a lot more of the world, but unfortunately, he could no longer travel due to his health complications.

Derek waited until he was dying to start living again. However, even though he received a second chance to die on his own terms, he was much too sad and depressed to enjoy anything at the very end. Life had become an empty existence for him once again. He became remorseful for the way he acted and would remind me that he understood that many others had terminal diseases. Strangely, he felt fortunate for getting the chance to try to be happy again, even if it was for a short time. Witnessing his sadness provided me with a much different perspective on life.

The far wing of our new house had been transformed into a hospital ward that housed Derek's hospital bed. His bedroom looked like an institution, with the steady flow of nurses and caregivers coming and going daily.

Sometimes, I would try to remember what life was like before Brandon was killed in 2012, but it seemed almost impossible. Our life back then felt as though it belonged to someone else, and I could barely remember it.

My relationship with Derek had now strictly become that of a caregiver/companion/nurse, and I had no recollection of a time it was not this way. At this point, a hug would cause Derek extreme pain as the cancer had reached every single one of his bones.

The role of caregiver is particularly torturous for an empath; I understood his pain much more than I wanted. I would silently wonder why life had been so relentlessly cruel to this family, first taking Brandon, then Devon, and leaving Derek to suffer a ravaging terminal illness.

I remember looking around Derek's room and seeing medication bottles and marijuana containers scattered all over. I often tried to organize his things, but he became strangely protective of knowing where everything was. His behavior was no longer making any sense, but since he had no control over his life, I didn't want to deny him anything.

The only promise Derek asked me to keep was that he wanted to die at home. Unfortunately, with his deteriorating condition, it became impossible. Even with twelve-hour nursing care daily, Derek was so intoxicated on Methadone he would crawl out of bed whenever someone would leave the room. I would later find him lying on the floor, disconnected from his IVs. In the end, the palliative care doctor told me to place Derek in hospice immediately.

Derek spent the next six weeks or so in hospice and had lost almost all ability to do anything. He couldn't even make a phone call home without assistance. Often, in the middle of the night, I would be woken up by the ringing of the telephone. When I'd pick up, all I'd hear would be the faint sound of Derek's breathing.

It was going to be Christmas Day in a couple of weeks, and it certainly did not feel like it this year. As much as possible, I tried to protect Christopher and Angelina from the pain of watching their father die, but the circumstances were devastating. After Devon's death, their relationship with him had become strained. Regardless, they would often go back and forth to his appointments and support him in his deteriorating state. It was especially hard for them to see their dad in the hospice at Christmas, but we did our best; life does not come with an instruction manual.

The hospice was decorated beautifully with a huge Christmas tree trimmed with red and gold. Christopher and Angelina had baked some Christmas cookies to bring to their dad. It always surprised me how good I felt going there—a strange thing of sorts to say, but there was a feeling of peace in the air. The volunteers were always in good spirits, and there was always something delicious baking in the oven. The smell of freshly baked cookies made me feel at ease.

A few days before Derek's death, he started to lose consciousness, and I felt it best the kids not see him that way. They said their final goodbyes then and didn't come back.

On December 13th, 2017, Derek passed away. I received the call and rushed to the hospice in the middle of the night, only to find him fully unconscious when I arrived. When you leave someone in hospice, you know each visit might be your last, so you make every visit count and say goodbye as though it is.

NEWS

Innisfil's Derek Majewski dies in hospice

By Rick Vanderlinde ✉ Innisfil Journal
Wednesday, December 20, 2017

Once Derek passed, it was safe to let go of the flood of emotions that had overwhelmed me for so long—the sadness, relief, pain, and disbelief. So much of this had been buried inside me, even though I always felt it bubbling just below the surface, threatening to overwhelm and crush me. I was now free to let everything out, and as the tears flowed like fire out of my body, something changed inside me, and I felt the room fill up with love and warmth. Although I couldn't see anyone, I felt like I was not alone. It was the most beautiful feeling I've felt in a long time. The sinking feeling of regret about not having the chance to say goodbye to Brandon and Devon was now gone.

As I sat in that room, many thoughts flashed through my mind, and I couldn't help but remember Devon's story about the "Majewski Curse," a curse he believed was his family's destiny. Was such a thing possible? I'm not sure, but if someone had told me in 2003 that the Majewski men would all be dead just a few short years after meeting them, I would have never believed it.

The Ripple Effect of Complicated Grief

Complicated grief is defined as the inability to let go of painful emotions surrounding loss, accompanied by the failure to resume daily responsibilities and activities. The effects of complicated grief can be devastating to both the sufferer and family.

When attempting to recover from grief, our physicians, psychologists, co-workers, and friends fiercely tried to free us from our pain. Often, people feel uncomfortable when others are in pain or "stuck." However, everyone grieves and recovers differently.

Watching someone drown in their emotions can be alarming. It can also be draining to try to help someone when nothing seems to work.

A lot of patience is required to heal a family after a significant loss, even if the family is intact and the love is strong.

The mind and body fight the pain as one is bombarded with mental and physical symptoms, including insomnia, oversleeping, nausea, headaches, weight loss or gain, alcohol and drug abuse, gambling addiction for a temporary high, overspending to fill the emptiness, etc.

The change in Derek's demeanor was so frightening that he was almost unrecognizable. Therefore, we only saw a handful of people outside of counselors. Because his moods were so unpredictable and unstable, we became very isolated and cut-off from the world.

The complicated grief that Derek experienced was unusual, extreme, and pathological. His grieving process for Brandon was disrupted by Devon's death, which was compounded by the ensuing pain of the lawsuit.

Derek's terminal illness diagnosis confirmed what I had believed all along—our minds can take a tremendous toll on our bodies, and that toll can manifest into physical illness.

Derek's therapists often told me that his state of mind was toxic and that on a quantum physics scale, he was vibrating very low. A high vibrational state is happy, compassionate, and peaceful, while a low vibrational state is associated with fear, anxiety, sadness, and depression.

It's hard not to let negative emotions take over and leave their mark, but it seems that our lives depend on it; the reality is that stress kills.

When it goes unresolved, stress can lead to chronic disease, causing premature death. The elevation of the stress hormone cortisol lowers immune system functioning, increases blood pressure, and cholesterol, and increases the risk of heart disease, cancer, and various other diseases.

However, grief doesn't last forever, despite how devastating and all-encompassing it can be. With the right help, support, and outlook, recovery will bring the body and mind to a new place of healing. We will never be the same again, but we will be stronger versions of ourselves. It's important to remember to approach recovery with some level of gratitude for the beauty of life—it's important to always express, accept, and learn from ourselves.

After Derek's funeral, I slept for a month straight and spoke to almost no-one aside from my sister-in-law, Judy, who graciously stayed with me and kept an eye on the house and kids. I barely remember the days or nights; my mind and body were depleted and absorbed all the uninterrupted sleep it could.

Picking up the Fragments

Living through the multiple deaths of my partner and step-children were by far the most painful years of my life, and recovery from grief was a long and ongoing journey full of heartbreak.

Beginning in 2016, I began to research trauma and the brain. I was now beginning to understand the connection between mind and body fully, and that dissociation was not a healthy coping mechanism, so I started taking rehabilitation seriously. Up to this point, I could only concentrate on my family as it seemed selfish to do otherwise, but it was now time to start helping myself and allowing others to do so as well.

One such person was Brianna, the owner of Compassionate Healing, a psychotherapy practice for children, adults, and survivors. Brianna had a background in social work and specialized in therapy with victims of trauma, assault, and grief. Her insight was incredible, and she took an approach to healing that went beyond traditional talk therapy; she introduced me to essential oils, yoga, meditation, and quantum psychics.

During one of our sessions, I remember her saying, "Derek is an empty vessel, and you need to protect yourself." I admit that it sounded strange at first, but then I understood. She explained that she could feel I was vibrating very high on a quantum physics level and that Derek was vibrating extremely low. She said he would unconsciously try to sabotage my healing if I did not protect myself internally.

It struck a chord in me, and I still think about it to this day when faced with a negative person. However, when the focus inside me turned to optimism instead of guilt, recovery instead of pain, and health instead of survival, everything for me changed.

Setting healthy boundaries while trying to heal without a significant other's participation, either because they are ill or they are just on a different page mentally, requires patience and compassion. We must understand that no good is going to come from allowing them to drain our energy. We must try to avoid giving too much if they are hurtful; the instinct is to try harder but we must not sink to their level. This can be especially hard to do with a spouse, but we must stay firm and clear with our boundaries and limits, and never threaten to leave. Since they are already feeling abandoned, threatening to leave them will only make things worse.

When we are ready for change and others are not, it doesn't mean we can't work on ourselves; it just needs to be done quietly since the other still deserves to be treated with love, dignity, and respect, even if they are agitating. Forgiveness goes a long way.

While there are many different therapy options to choose from, the point is to have and accept support; we don't want to travel this path alone, as the fear, pain, shock, and sadness can be overwhelming.

I have tried and experienced years of traditional talk therapy (IPT), hypnotherapy, emotional freedom technique sessions, cognitive behavioral therapy (CBT), acupuncture, acupressure, practicing mindfulness and meditation in groups and on my own, as well as various types of yoga, including restorative yoga instruction and classes.

Yoga can help promote relaxation, stress relief, encourage us to live in the moment, and, most importantly, it forces us to slow down and breathe.

Yoga helped me over the years in the most extraordinary of ways. I have been practicing yoga, gymnastics, and Pilates all my life, but I have found yoga unbelievably helpful with trauma.

In Western society, we mainly practice yoga as a form of physical exercise. Regular practice provides physiological benefits such as flexibility, strength, muscle relaxation, and healthy organ function, but practicing yoga also provides emotional, mental, and spiritual benefits.

We tend to hold emotions in specific parts of the body. Your lower back, for example, is the foundation for your body. So, if you are experiencing lower back problems, then it is likely that you will experience feelings such as fear, worry, insecurity, or instability. Alternatively, if you are going through a time in your life where you are insecure or apprehensive, you may experience lower back discomfort.

When you have digestive problems, it may be that you are having trouble processing current issues in your life. How many times have you felt "nauseous" when you received bad news or felt "your heart sink" when you were distressed because you felt this sensation happening in your body?

Your physical body is intrinsically tied to your emotional state. Therefore, by practicing yoga, we can control our mental state in a very positive way.

Practicing yoga will help you feel more whole as if every part of your body is functioning in a connected way.

I have been practicing yoga for years, but I didn't realize the profound effects it had on my physical and emotional well-being until I abruptly stopped when tragedy struck. My body rebelled in the most profound ways, but I didn't notice the change until I started practicing again.

Below are the seven poses that you can do at home for grief:

Balasana (Child's Pose)

This posture encapsulates what the body organically wants to do when we are under duress: curl inward. Come onto your shins with the tops of the feet on the floor. Bring your big toes together and spread your knees apart. Shift your hips back toward your heels and reach your arms in front of you. Rest your forehead on a block to give your brain a rest. It helps to be on your fingertips to keep space in your neck and shoulders. Stay here as long as you like.

Sukhasana (Comfortable Pose)

Continue to rest your brain while starting to release your hips. Because the body contracts after trauma, long holds are a gentle way to start to open things back up. Start by sitting on your mat or a folded blanket. Cross your legs so that your right shin is in front of your left, resting your knees on your ankles. Flex your ankles strongly to protect your knees. On an inhalation, reach your arms up to the ceiling; on an exhalation, fold over your legs, resting your forehead on a block or the floor. Stay here for 25 long breaths. Inhale to slowly come up and switch sides.

Uttanasana (Standing Forward Fold)

Reconnect to your legs and, as a result, your strength with this calming and lengthening forward fold. At the back of the mat, step your feet hip-width distance apart, and on an exhalation, fold over your legs. If you are able, rest the crown of your head on a block, which can be incredibly restorative. Otherwise, simply let your head hang. Your arms will dangle loosely, palms on the floor, or clasp opposite elbows. Hold for 15 breaths. Round your way to standing, very slowly, one vertebra at a time. Let your head be the last thing to come up and stand upright for a few moments before moving on to the next pose.

Parsvottanasana (Pyramid Pose)

Begin by standing at the front of your mat, then exhale and step your left foot back about 3 feet. Turn your back foot inward about 45 degrees for stability; your feet should be slightly wider than heel to heel. Place your hands on your hips, and on an inhalation, lift your chest; on an exhalation, fold over your legs, putting your hands on blocks or the floor. If your arms are long enough, you may walk your hands back toward your back foot. Lengthen your torso over your front leg by reaching your chest to the front foot. Stay here for 20 breaths. On an inhalation, come halfway up; on an exhalation, bring your hands to your hips. Inhale all the way up to standing and step your back foot to the top of the mat to repeat on the other side.

Janu Sirsasana (Head to Knee Pose)

This simple pose is incredibly comforting because, in this pose, you'll rest upon yourself. Start seated on a blanket with both of your legs straight out in front of you.

Bend your right knee and turn your thigh open, pulling your right heel up toward your groin. On an inhalation, reach your arms up to the sky and exhale fold over the left thigh. You may grab an opposite wrist (in this case, right hand holds left wrist) or simply bend your elbows on the floor. Disregard the name of the pose, and instead of trying to touch your head to your knee, which can lead to over-rounding, think of reaching the top of your head to your foot. Stay here for 30 breaths, and on an inhalation, come up to sit. Stretch your right leg out and pause before switching sides.

Restorative Paschimottanasana (Western Stretch)

Go even further inward with this back-body lengthener. This pose releases not only your back thighs, but also your postural muscles, which work so hard to keep our head up when we are in grief or suffering. Sitting on your mat or a folded blanket, separate your legs as wide as your hips. Place a block between your legs, closer to your shins. On an inhalation, reach your arms up; on an exhalation, fold over both legs. Flip the block as high as it needs to be in order to rest your forehead on it. Your arms can rest by your sides with your elbows bent, which releases the muscles of your upper back, or you may reach to grab your feet. Take 30 breaths here before slowly inhaling to come up with a long spine.

Savasana (Corpse Pose)

Savasana is quite a vulnerable shape in the best of times, so we will use a blanket to continue the feeling of being protected while gently opening the body and ourselves back up to the outer world. You can use as light or as heavy a blanket as feels comfortable. Lay on your back and separate your legs slightly wider than your hips, allowing your thighs to roll open. Place a folded blanket over your chest and belly, with the top of the blanket at the height of your shoulders. Let your arms rest by your sides and turn your palms so that they face upward. Let this be a symbol of starting to take in the energy of the outside world. Rest the back of your head against the mat and keep your eyes closed and brain heavy. Stay here for 7 to 10 minutes. When it is time to come out, move very slowly. Let this symbolize how gentle you will be with yourself during this delicate time. On an inhalation, raise your arms overhead, bend your knees, and roll to your right side. Stay here in the fetal position for a minute or longer, then press into the floor with your left hand and come up to sit on an inhalation. Your head should be the last thing to rise. Sit quietly with yourself for a few minutes, simply allowing any emotions to arrive.

This sequence of poses was my godsend in helping me deal with my overwhelming emotions, keeping my feet on the ground and my head in my body.

I hope this helps you as well. Namaste.

Cognitive behavior therapy (CBT) and eye movement desensitization and reprocessing (EMDR) can be very effective for PTSD, grief, and trauma.

The basis of CBT is to help build skills to become more aware of our thoughts and emotions, identify how our thoughts and behaviors influence our emotions, and improve our feelings by changing our dysfunctional thoughts and behaviors. This helps us become more aware of our negative thoughts, many of which have become ingrained in our thought patterns.

Cognitive restructuring is the basis for CBT. It is a psychotherapeutic process that helps us identify and dispute irrational thoughts by deconstructing them and rebuilding them in a more balanced and accurate way. By doing so, we can see both sides of the situation and have a more balanced perspective.

CBT works to undo unhelpful and damaging thinking patterns. This process is ideal if it can be done with a therapist, as objective observations help identify unhealthy thought patterns. Once the process of CBT is understood, this practice can be done alone. I still practice it subconsciously; it has become part of the way I think without realizing it.

EMDR is an interactive psychotherapy technique that is widely used for various disorders, including PTSD, eating disorders, substance abuse, complicated grief, panic, dissociative disorders, and many other disorders associated with trauma. During EMDR therapy sessions, the patient recalls a traumatic experience while the therapist directs the patient's eye movements. It is believed that EMDR works because the "bilateral stimulation" bypasses the area of the brain that has become stuck due to trauma, preventing the left side of the brain from self-soothing the right side of the brain.

It is my sincere hope that sharing my therapy experiences may help shorten someone's grief. I understand how lonely, isolating, unbearable, and soul-sucking the pain can be.

The most important thing to remember is to take it one day at a time. Eat nutritious whole foods, exercise daily, enjoy nature, seek the help of a counselor, practice mindfulness. Carving out a little bit of time to do something for yourself every day will help you feel recharged.

Life is short; try to find your smile again and find joy and appreciation in the here and now.

Present Day

The strongest emotion that I feel today is unmistakably gratitude. I am grateful to be alive, healthy, stable, and loved.

On a sunny day in January 2018, I woke up and suddenly felt different. What happened to me next can only be described as enlightenment or a spiritual awakening. I felt an indescribable lightness in my body and mind and felt as though something had died and was reborn inside me. The world outside looked different, and all at once, I felt excited to be alive. The warm feeling of gratitude that swept over me was unmistakable, and I wanted to join the world again. The guilt, sadness, depression, and anxiety I had been harboring for so many years was gone, and I was instead flooded with a deep sense of peace and bliss that has not left me since.

I had forgotten what it meant to be happy, but I knew right then and there that I did not want to waste another moment of this precious life. I wanted to start fresh and close the door to my past for good; I wanted to rise from the ashes like a Phoenix and take the world on anew.

Immediately, new people came into my life as though through divine intervention, and I felt inspired. The gratitude I felt in my heart translated into a gravitational pull, drawing powerfully positive people in.

I closed the door on the past, and the new doors automatically opened, one of which led me to Scott, a retired entrepreneur and the incredibly handsome, compassionate, and emotionally intelligent man in my life today. We felt an immediate connection from the moment we met, and even though I couldn't comprehend it, I knew the universe was intervening.

Love is especially sweet when it comes to us when we least expect it. I certainly was not expecting it, and I was completely swept off my feet in the most magical way. Scott and I were immediately drawn to one another with such force that it felt as though we had known each other all our lives. His warmth, depth and kindness touched my heart, and I immediately felt at peace.

I was not expecting to find my soulmate, so I feel blessed that the universe brought us together and feel such gratitude.

What happened to Brandon the night of October 28th, 2012 and the events that followed have forever changed my life, giving me a newfound appreciation for what it means to be alive. I will cherish the memory of the three Majewski men—Derek, Devon, and Brandon—in my heart forever. They have made me into the person I am today, and I will be eternally grateful to them. My intent is not for Brandon, Devon, and Derek to be defined by the tragedies of their deaths; instead, my aspiration is to have the truth set them free. May they rest in peace.

THE END

I wish to give credit and acknowledgement to the amazing Journalists whose diligence and passion were so instrumental in assisting the family in our search for the truth, your commitment and support were so appreciated.

Special thanks goes to Rick Vanderline @ The Innisfil Journal, Tracy McLaughlin and Ian McInroy @ The Toronto Sun, Mike Walker @ CTV News Barrie, Simcoe.com as well as Larry Hurd and Laurie Budd for all that you did.

About the Author

- -

Lisa Dianne McInnes has always been fascinated with spirituality and the human experience. She prides herself on always being committed to the truth, even when it hurts, and believes in being reliable, trustworthy, honest, and loyal to those she loves.

However, in 2012, when tragedy struck and shattered her family, Lisa's beliefs were tested and she was forced to undergo a profound inner transformation. In doing so, she had to acknowledge the trauma of her past but chose only to remember the love her family shared. Her solid understanding and belief in the theory of mindfulness and living in the moment helped her rise from the ashes and move on with her life. She believes the past can be like a black hole: if you stand too close it will pull you in,

Today, small things like sunsets, staring out at the water, and kisses for no reason are the reasons she smiles. She believes it is the simple memories that define us, and the ones we hold close to our hearts. For Lisa, writing allows her to share her struggles and experiences with others, and by doing so she learns and grows both mentally and spiritually through the process. Therefore, with her work, she hopes to inspire her readers to join her on the journey to find inner peace and greater fulfillment in their lives.

Lisa completed her debut novel, The Majewski Curse, and is currently preparing to start writing her second non-fiction work. She currently resides in Northern Ontario with her spouse and their puppy Cooper.

Manufactured by Amazon.ca
Bolton, ON

20478512R00081